MY FOLK

Four hundred years of Hazards, Tooths, and Connellys

Jim Connelly

BY THE SAME AUTHOR

Children's fiction

Tom and Anna on the Trail: the Case of the Missing Schoolgirl

Tom and Anna in Danger: the Case of the Disappearing Dogs

Tom and Anna take a Chance: the Case of the Bungling Bird Bandits

MY FOLK

Four hundred years of Hazards, Tooths, and Connellys

Copyright

Copyright Jim Connelly 2015

Paperback ISBN: 978-0-9924547-6-0

All rights reserved.

No part of this publication may be reproduced or transmitted in any form or by any means, electronic or mechanical, including photocopying, recording, or any information storage and retrieval system, without prior permission in writing of the copyright owner.

A CIP catalogue record for this book is available from the National Library of Australia.

First Published in Australia 2015
By
James Timothy Connelly
10 Stoddarts Road
Warragul Victoria 3820
AUSTRALIA

ajcon@dcsi.net.au

For Anne

MY FOLK

Four hundred years of Hazards, Tooths, and Connellys

Jim Connelly

CONTENTS

Foreword — 9

Starter — 13

PART 1. SHAMROCK — 16

    James Connelly's Story — 21

    William Francis Connelly's Story — 31

Part 2. ROSE — 55

    Thomas Hazard's Story — 56

    Joyce Winifred Hazard's Story — 69

PART 3. WATTLE — 120

    James Timothy Connelly's Story — 121

FOREWORD

These pages represent my duty to the Hazard, Tooth, and Connelly families, in particular. They are the rootstock of the twenty-first century Australian Connelly family.

On the Hazard and Tooth side, many documents and photographs came to me from my aunt, Rosalind Hazard, on her death, and she had many of those from her father, Henry Hazard, who made a determined effort in the 1890s to establish his family tree, which he called, after the fashion of the time, his pedigree. I also reached back to generations past through my cousins, Rachael Corkill and Rosalind Heinz, and my niece, Phillippa Connelly, and through others. The Tooths enter the story at a relatively late stage, but have played a major role in the family legend over the last hundred and fifty years.

With the Connellys, there was no parallel regarding documentation, although birth, marriage and death certificates and war service records helped, as did a variety of photographs many of which somehow ended up with me. Mary McMahon, a cousin, was able to tell of many personal details of the generations above me, and other family members, both close and distant, helped in many ways, particularly my sister, Angela Costain, and my brother, Noel Connelly.

Several people have given great help with the production of this book, notably, again, my brother, Noel Connelly, who drew up the family trees with his magnificent calligraphy, Nigel Beresford who converted the photographs into the correct format for publication, and, above all, Mark Biggs who assisted me through the technical side of getting the book into print from the first beginnings right through to the end.

The story is presented through five voices, though the words are mine. There are imaginative reconstructions in several places. Some puzzles remain, but I am sure these will be solved with further research. The principal one is how and when James Connelly and Catherine O'Neil journeyed to Australia. There were several James Connellys who arrived from Ireland at about the right time, and several Catherine O'Neils too, allowing for variant spellings in each case. But which were the right ones? Was our James Connelly the crewman of that name who came on a ship from New Zealand? Or the 'J. Connelly' who attended a church meeting in Learmonth as early as 1857? I present the best of my knowledge and memory at the present time, and I look forward to the revisions and additions that other people will make. Much has been omitted in the interests of brevity, and there is more to be discovered by diligent research about almost every individual mentioned in the text.

Memories can, of course, be misleading. No set of memoirs is perfectly reliable. Much of the later history here is from my memory; it may differ from others' memories. There is a good deal of interpretation written into the text, and it may be that others will not agree with some of it. This applies to many individual comments, but also to the major theme of the whole work, which is unstated, but which, I think, may be easily identified.

I have entitled this record 'My Folk' to emphasise that although many have helped in putting it together, it is written from my own point of view. Perhaps because of this, the whole work begins in relatively general fashion and becomes more and more oriented towards my own immediate family as it goes on.

Jim Connelly,
Warragul,
March, 2015.

STARTER

'I don't think you can call it coincidence that I was born,' I said.

'Cigarette stop!' Dad announced. I must have said something which made one of his mini-lectures shoot out from the filing cabinet.

He parked on a hill with a splendid view of the Adriatic.

'Sit down!' he ordered when we were out of the car, and pointed to a large stone.

'Thirteen forty-nine,' was the first thing he said.

'The Black Death,' I replied. I had a pretty good knowledge of history, but I had no idea what the Black Death had to do with coincidences.

'Okay,' he said, and off he went. 'You probably know that half Norway's population was wiped out during the Great Plague …'.

When he began like this, I knew it was going to be a long lecture.

'Did you know that you had thousands of ancestors at that time?' he continued.

I shook my head in despair. How could that possibly be?

'You have two parents, four grandparents, eight great-grandparents, sixteen great-great-grandparents – and so on. If you work it out, right back to 1349 – there are quite a lot.'

I nodded.

'Then came the bubonic plague. Death spread from neighbourhood to neighbourhood, and the children were worst hit. Whole families died, sometimes one or two family members survived. A lot of your ancestors were children at that time, Hans Thomas. But none of *them* kicked the bucket.'

'How can you be so sure about that?' I asked in amazement.

He took a drag on his cigarette and said, 'Because you're sitting here looking out over the Adriatic.'

Once again he had made such an astounding point I didn't really know how to respond. But I knew he was right, because if just one of my ancestors had died as a child, then he wouldn't have been my ancestor.

'The chances of one single ancestor of yours not dying while growing up is one in several billion,' he went on, and now the words flowed out of him like a waterfall. 'Because it isn't just about the Black Death, you know. Actually *all* your ancestors have grown up and had children – even during the worst of the natural disasters, even when the child mortality rate was enormous. Of course, a lot of them suffered from illness, but they've always pulled through. In a way, you have been a millimetre away from death billions of times, Hans Thomas. Your life on this planet has been threatened by insects, wild animals, meteorites, lightning, sickness, war, floods, fires, poisonings, and attempted murders. In the Battle of Stiklestad alone you were injured hundreds of times. Because you must have had ancestors on both sides – yes, really you were fighting against yourself and your chances of being born a thousand years later. You know, the same goes for the last war. If Grandpa had been shot by good Norwegians during the occupation, then neither you nor I would have been born. The point is, this has happened billions of times through history. Each time an arrow has rained through the air, *your* chances of being born have been reduced to the minimum. But here you are, sitting talking to me, Hans Thomas! Do you see?'

'I think so,' I said.

Jostein Gaarder, The Solitaire Mystery, 1996; Phoenix, London, pp 116-7

PART 1. SHAMROCK

CHAPTER 1

The baptism party was in the smithy. For the warmth.

Tim pumped the bellows till the coals glowed and sparkled. Annie brought oatcakes and a jug from her kitchen and set them on the work bench covered now with a linen cloth. The baby slept in a cot Timothy himself had made.

It was November, 1836 - a hard year for County Kilkenny. The cold weather had set in early. The potato crop was savaged by leaf curl and dry rot.

Times were perhaps a little better in Graiguenamanagh than elsewhere. The river was important to the town. Not far from here the Barrow joins the Nore and flows down to the sea at Waterford. Barges carried grain, manure, wood, and sugar beet, and brought some business to the town – and in a small way to Timothy Connelly's smithy.

Tim and his family, of course, belonged to the old Faith. Of the 5000 in Graiguenamanagh, there were ninety-nine Catholics for every Protestant. But the English Protestants were dominant. Despite Catholic Emancipation seven years earlier, tithes were still exacted on all citizens for the upkeep of the clergy of the established Church of England. These tithes were payable in cash or kind, usually the latter. The payment of tithes was a deep wound in the hearts of Irish Catholics.

Five years earlier, in 1831, the first uprising against the imposition of tithes had taken place here at Graiguenamanagh. The hero was the Parish Priest, Father Doyle. By custom, tithes were not levied on clergy with small holdings of land. Father Doyle gathered everyone's cattle together and declared they were his. Trouble broke out, but bloodshed was averted. Rebellions did break out in other places. Dozens of local people died, and some of the constabulary also.

The parish church was Duiske Abbey, standing in the middle of the town. The Abbey had not long been handed back to the Catholics after 150 years of Protestant occupation. It was once one of the finest Cistercian abbeys in Ireland.

* * *

The baptism followed morning Mass at the Abbey.

The handful of babies, the gaggle of parents and children, all dressed in their best clothes, were dwarfed by the ornate building around them.

Father Doyle conducted the service, then blessed and dismissed the gathering.

Tim, with Annie carrying their new baby, walked from the building, past the two ancient stone crosses, and hurried to their home a short distance away. Tim unlocked the narrow door and they entered the living space of the house. The sleeping room was adjacent, the kitchen and washing room being at the rear of the building. Another door in the front room gave direct access to the forge, although it had its own entrance off the street, with a wide swing door to allow for the entry of horses and small vehicles.

At two o'clock, three families arrived to share the baptismal celebration. They all lived close by. One of the fathers was a farm labourer, one worked at the salt works, while the third had a job at the wharf. Tim swung open the main forge door to admit them. The adults stood around the glowing coals in the furnace; the children sat desultorily on the floor. There were no seats.

After some time there was a knocking at the door, and a pleased look crossed Timothy's face. He hurried to swing the door open.

"Ah! I knew you'd come, Father,' he said as the parish priest entered.

'I've blessed the baby,' he replied. 'Now I must bless the family.'

'We're honoured to have you christen the boy,' Tim went on. 'For all time, he can be proud that Father Doyle of great fame was his christener.'

'Not so much of that,' said Father Doyle. 'I pray that the great fame will belong to him.'

Annie passed the cakes around while Timothy poured measures of poteen into tin flasks. Everyone stood expectantly in a circle.

Father Doyle stepped forward. 'To the man of the hour,' he declared and raised his flask. 'God bless him, wherever life may take him. We drink to the future of ... James Connelly.'

CHAPTER 2

JAMES CONNELLY

I am that baby. James Connelly, first child of Timothy and Annie Connelly, whose name before she was married I don't know.

It is now 1916, and I have eighty years to tell you of.

I've always been fit and strong, and I got off to a fair start in life, I have to say. I was at school quite a bit. The National School, brand-new it was, and classes free, but I never was one for my letters, and I stayed away much of the time. My dad needed me in the forge. I'd hold the horses while he shod them, or worked the bellows when I was larger, or passed him his tools when he was on a difficult job. And I'd mind the young ones when ma was sick. I did learn to write my name, and could do a fair job of it, though I never was good at joining those letters together.

I think when you're the oldest in the family you have a hard row to hoe, but it did me good just the same. I was a man when I was still a boy. My dad called me his apprentice, though he never signed papers to that effect, and I never was a proper-trained blacksmith, though I know the trade as well as any man. The brothers, they got jobs round about after they were done with the school, though none of the jobs amounted to much.

Then came that terrible year when the Black Famine came across from France in 1845. I was just a boy. The potatoes went bad and the people got sick or died. A good number of people went away. To America and places. But I was only nine or ten at the time, and there was no chance of us going, though my dad would often talk about it. There was always a bit of work for him. People have to have shoes on their horses and wheels on their carts. We stuck it out, but the news kept coming from America of the Kilkenny boys over there, and it never was out of my mind that one day I'd give it a crack.

The years went past and Ma and Pa kept going on in the old way. It put me into a dark time. All I could think of was me being left at home with the old folk, while those other Kilkenny lads would be kicking over the traces somewhere in the sun. It worked on me day and night. I looked at my dad. He was no better off than the day he was born. The only thing he owned were his tools, and they weren't much. Then I'd think they needed me, the old ones, but Pa was still strong and Ma was able to help him, except for the horses.

So one day it came to me in a rush. I wasn't going to be put in the shade by those others. I would go too, but I would go one better than them. I told Pa one day and he went red with anger. Ma cried, but I was determined by then to go, and having spoken to them about it, it seemed to make it all easier.

So I sent off to go to Australia.

CHAPTER 3

I can't think now of the name of the ship, but I know I went down to Cork, and then to Liverpool and we sailed from there. It cost me six pounds, I remember.

A lot of families were on board, but there were some young people which made it more interesting. Not that there was much jawing at all. I kept myself to myself most of the time, though towards the end I got in with some of the others. After I'd got my ground legs working I went by coach to Ballarat, where the talk was that though the gold was giving out, there was still good work about. This was near sixty year ago so my memory is dim about some of those doings. I got into the blacksmithing trade when a chance came up at Learmonth, fifteen miles out from Ballarat. Without going into every nook and cranny, it worked out that by the time a few years had gone, I had the smithy in Learmonth in my own right and had put down the money on a place two miles from there, at Weatherboard Hill. Just a few acres with a wretched old place on it, but I wasn't used to much at home, so didn't expect much here. I still live on that land, I'm proud to say, and I've added to it over the years.

There was a girl up there, servanting in a big place nearby, and we hit it off pretty well. Her name was Cath O'Neil, and she was fresh out from Ireland, too, but from County Clare in her case. Cath and I decided to make a go of it together. We went to see

Father Sheil in Ballarat and fixed the date for Sunday afternoon, the twenty-sixth of October at Saint Alipius'. 1862, that is.

* * *

Father Sheil was an old Irishman, and I know he wasn't very popular later on, after they made him a bishop, when he put that Mary Mackillop out of the Church, but he was kind to us.

After the service we had to sign the papers.

'How should you be spelling your name with an 'e'?' Father Sheil said to me. 'All the Connallys I know put an 'a' in the middle.' And that's what he made me put, though I've used the proper way – with an 'e' – ever since.

'Now, Kate,' he said to Catherine, 'you sign your name there.' Cath went red in the face. 'I can't,' she whispered. She'd been too nervous to tell him she couldn't write. But he was very good about it and wrote her name in himself, and got her to put her cross between the two names, 'Catherine O'Neil.'

John Shanahan and Margaret Dunnovan stood for us. Father laughed when it turned out they had to put their marks as well. He thought it was funny that I was the only one of us who could write their name. I'm glad Father didn't ask me to write anything else!

He wanted to know everything about us and wrote it in the certificate. He said the Government needed to know. He wrote down where we came from back home and where we lived now, and about our parents. I told him about my ma and pa, and Catherine told him how her father was Patrick O'Neil, and that he was a farmer in County Clare, and that her mother's name before she was married was Margaret Casey.

Looking back on it all, I have a bit of a laugh. There we were, all of us Irish. It was as if we were just playing at being Australian.

CHAPTER 4

Learmonth was just getting started when we came here. The first blocks had been surveyed a few years earlier, and houses were starting to be built along the main road. Before we'd hardly settled in, there were three other blacksmiths besides ourselves. Things got tight and I was glad I'd got that bit of land to run a few cattle on.

I did some stupid things in the early days, before we were married. I was up before the beak once or twice. They held the Court right next to the Police Station, so if the police ran you in, you wouldn't get much joy from the JPs. That's what the gossip was.

One time I went on a bit of a spree with a mate of mine, Paddy Kennelly. We were both done for drunk and disorderly, and we thought we were in for a hard time when it turned out that old Learmonth himself was on the bench that day. They wrote it up in the paper, unfortunately for us.

'Patrick Kennelly,' he said, after he had listened to the police side of things, 'what have you got to say?'

'Nothing, your Worship,' says Paddy, 'but it's the first time I've been here.'

'Indeed,' says the old man, 'and if I see you here again, I'll double your fine. Ten shillings to be paid before release.'

Then he turns to me. 'Anything from you, Connelly?' he says. 'No Sir,' I says back to him.

'I think your friend led you astray,' he announces. 'Keep away from him,' he tells me. 'Discharged without conviction,' and he steps down.

Paddy was crooked on me for getting off like that, but we had another drink on the old bloke, and he felt better after that.

I had some trouble another couple of times. This was later on, when we were on the home block at Weatherboard and I was trying to make a go of it, running some cattle and selling them to the fatteners. It was a real bad summer. Those bush fires came through only a couple of months later, at the end of February 1866, it must have been. Well, we were pretty much out of feed, and there were some good pickings down on the lake foreshore, in the recreation reserve. So I let the cattle through there once or twice, and somebody must have reported on me, because I was taken up and fined for it. I can laugh at it now, but it hurt at the time.

Another time I was in court I was on the right side of the law. I used to do a bit of work round the district when it was about and I could spare the time. I did some jobs for John Robinson who ran the *Rose, Thistle, and Shamrock* over at Mount Blowhard, and never got what was due to me, so I took him up, and the magistrate found for me. I got something over three pounds, and five bob costs! The blighter never gave me any more work, though!

Learmonth was getting to be a busy place. The *Stag* was the main place in the town, especially at the weekends. The McKenzies had it for a long time - fifty or sixty years, altogether. They got a lot of business because of it being the coaching depot as well as the hotel. The ploughing matches were held there, too, and people came from all round the district for those, and from New South Wales and South Australia as well.

Some folk used to come out from Ballarat because of the lake. In summer, they'd have regattas on the weekends. When the train came through - that was later, in the 'eighties - there would be day specials out to Learmonth for the boat races. The train was good for us, too, for getting into Ballarat for the day.

Everybody knew each other in those days. Creelman was the doctor – Creelman, with his Scottish accent. He was the doctor when the children were born. He had a big property, too. Diphtheria was the thing we worried about. When we first came to Learmonth, people were still talking about the diphtheria that came through a few years before. There was a family called Longmore lived on the lake. The parents died, both of them, and seven of the nine children. It got in the papers, how the uncle wouldn't let the doctor near the two little ones. He said it was the doctoring that killed the others.

I won't go through them all now, and I may be a bit mixed up about which ones were here when, but I'll mention one or two. There was McGlashans had the engineering works and did a bit of blacksmithing as well, against me. Old McGlashan invented that reaper everyone used to use. Must have made a fortune from it. Walker came in there after him. He got kicked by a horse and had his leg amputated. Fraser was another who did blacksmithing, and Lugg, too, though he did most of his work with the coaches and wagons. There was Mackay, as well, for a bit.

Tom Barnes had the timber-yard. He made all the coffins, and finished up doing the undertaking as well. Bob Pool was the saddler for years till Bill Sara took over. We'd often send bits of harness down to him to be fixed up. He was something of a mate of mine, Bill Sara, and I got him to witness my will a few years ago. Hedrick was in the store in the early times, but Bill McKay had it for a long time, till he sold out to Spiers. The Dunrobin Store, they called it. Tom Lowe was the baker and he'd bring the bread out to the farm. Same with the meat - Alf Sandland early on, then the Rasdells. Richmond was the teacher at the Weatherboard School, till he gave it up to become Shire Secretary. That's where the young ones went to school. Very handy, just down the hill.

The Boxing Day sports was the biggest thing in town. Run by the Agricultural Society. They were mostly novelty events, as they called them, but there were high jumps and running races, too. Some of the younger ones went in for those and won prizes. They were pretty fast, some of the boys – and some of the grandchildren as well. Catch the greasy pig was always the last event, and then the dance at night.

A lot of men from round here used to go over and get work on Ercildoune, Learmonth's' place. 20, 000 odd acres. He sold out to Wilson about forty year ago. Sir Samuel Wilson. There was great goings on that time when Jack Gowrie held the place up. That was the day! Everybody was talking about it. They shot him, of course. Shot him dead there on Ercildoune Hill. It was Wilson that leased the place to Nellie Melba, just a few years ago. There was plenty of talk about that, too!

There were nine children born to us over those years. Will was the first, and after him there was Jim, then Maggie, Pat, Tim, Michael, Richard, Mary Ann, and Catherine. Sixteen years covered the lot of them. Now, some of them have got their own children. I won't tell of them now. I'll leave that to the next generation to report on.

Here I am, an old man, and you'd hope I would have that large family to be a comfort to me. In fact my wife has been gone these many years, and of those nine children, only five are left. Perhaps I've lived too long.

CHAPTER 5

WILLIAM FRANCIS CONNELLY

My grandfather, James Connelly, died in March, 1916, after nearly sixty years in Learmonth, if you count Weatherboard as part of that town.

I'm Will, as I'm known. William Francis Connelly. You may think it's odd that I begin by speaking of my grandfather rather than my own father or mother, but the truth is that he meant more to me than my parents did.

You have to say that old Jim – my grandfather – did pretty well with his life. He could hardly write, and he never read hardly a thing all his life, and I know he had a scratchy start to life out here, but it finished that people looked up to him all round the district and he was the main one in our family. When he died it was written up in the paper. They had the heading 'Pioneer's Death' and this is what it said:

> *The oldest resident of the Learmonth district in the person of Mr James Connelly passed away on Wednesday at the ripe age of 80 years. Born in Kilkenny, Ireland, Mr Connelly came to Australia in the 1850s and settled in Learmonth, and for a number of years carried on a blacksmithing*

> business. Afterwards he took up a farm at Weatherboard, where he has lived ever since. Mr Connelly leaves a grown-up family of four sons and one daughter.

They still call the place out there at Weatherboard 'Connelly's Corner.' The old place is gone. It was hardly fit to live in at the end. It was so dark and damp, with the brick floor in the kitchen all sagging, and the sheds no better. My Uncle Pat pulled it down and burnt it. He bought a big house from the Burrumbeet racecourse and put it up there. A fine big house it was, four bedrooms and a big drawing room. They called it 'Tullamore' from my grandmother, Annie, coming from Tulla in Ireland. But even it's gone now, and there's only some of the old pine trees left to mark the place.

Old Jim, my grandfather, left the farm to my Uncle Pat. He and his sister, Aunt Maggie, were the ones who stayed with him there, and looked after him. He was worth a bit when he died, the old man. There was the land – more than sixty acres when you put it all together – and the horses and cattle, and all the bits and pieces. He was running sixteen head of cattle at the end, that Pat took over. It was all valued because of his will, and, with the money he had in the Bank, it came to one thousand, seven hundred pounds. I was never one to care much about property and money, but you've got to say that he did all right, especially when he came out here with nothing at all.

The site of the original Connelly homestead at Weatherboard

I've been reading what my grandfather wrote up above, He didn't want to say anything about his family, so I'll tell you what I can. My grandmother, Catherine O'Neil she was before she was married, died in 1909, a couple of days before Christmas, when I was seventeen. I remember her in that big old house, almost falling down. She didn't get about much, especially in winter because of her bronchitis, though she had friends, like Mrs Dalgliesh. It was a funny thing how they got on. Old Dalgliesh – Andrew - had a big place a bit further out, running sheep. Scottish and Presbyterian and lots of money. Mrs Dalgliesh would come up the road at night, in the dark often, and sit with my grandmother when she was ill in bed with the bronchitis, they'd talk away there for hours. I listened to them one night. Mrs Dalgliesh said, 'Just as well you're not married to my lousy old husband.' And my grandmother said back to her, 'You ought to try living with my bad-tempered old Irishman!' She was in bed half the year with her bronchitis, the old woman, and got weaker and weaker towards the end. On the death certificate, the doctor called it heart failure and senile decay. My grandfather went the same way. "Acute degeneration of the heart," they said. Still, at eighty, what do you expect?

* * *

To get back to my father's family. Will was the oldest. That's my dad. He married Cecilia Curran at St. Alipius' in Ballarat, same as my grandparents. That was 1891, in November. Will's brother, Jim, stood witness for him, and, on Cissie's side, her sister, Annie. I've worked out from the dates that I was born five months later, so it was a case of them having to get married, not that they ever said anything about that to me, and I won't say much about them just now either. I'll tell about our family a bit later on. I'll stick with the generation above me for now.

My Uncle Jim – James, really – was born second, after my father. He was the one who went to Western Australia. He came back only the once. I remember him, a big, tall man, with a grey suit, which wasn't very common round these parts. No one at Weatherboard had seen him for twenty or thirty years.

He just walked in one day. He was very well-behaved. Never swore. He was always saying, 'Well, by scissors, eh?' Some of us used to call him 'Uncle Scissors.' He was very nice to talk to. After a while he went back to the West and never came this way again. After he died over there, a letter came from a lady, not his wife. He never married. She said that Jim had told her that after he died she should come to Weatherboard because his brothers and sisters would look after her. And she wanted money, too. My Aunt Maggie hit the roof. She wrote back and said no; she and Pat were on the pension!

Then there was Maggie who came after Jim. Margaret was her grandmother's name on her mother's side. Maggie never married. After her father, old Jim, died, she and her brother, Pat, stayed on at the old place. She and Pat, they were the two. They kept the family together. Very loyal to their mother and father. It seemed a shame that the old man left the farm to Uncle Pat alone, but I suppose it didn't matter so much. When Pat died, Maggie went to live with her niece, my sister Annie, at Waubra. Annie was married to Bill Gallagher by then.

Pat was next after Maggie. He was small and quiet, and a terrible tease to us younger ones, but a really good man. He and Maggie were very strong for their parents and for the old place at Weatherboard Hill. Others came and went, but they were always there. They were quite shrewd in their own way. They bought a couple of other blocks, and they used to rent a bit of land – several different paddocks not too far away. One of them was Ryan's Paddock, they used to call it. Then they worked Mrs Morgan's place on shares at one time. They used to get people to work for them, like Billy Dowler. Pat had a weak chest, same as his mother, and died when he was sixty-two. It was good that when Maggie died later on, she was buried with Pat, the two of them together.

My father's Uncle Pat (left) and Uncle Tim, with young Pat Ryan between them. Pat and Tim were the fourth and fifth children of James and Catherine Connelly, the original Connelly settlers in Australia. Pat Ryan married their sister's daughter, Maggie. The photo is taken at the original Connelly house at Weatherboard, which can be seen in the background. The pine trees still stands at 'Connelly's Corner'. Weatherboard

My father's Aunt Maggie, known to the family as simply 'Aunt'. She and her brother, Pat, were the ones who kept the family together. Maggie died in 1950

After that there was Tim, named after his grandfather back in Ireland. Tim was different from the others. In some ways it was like he was a real Connelly, but there was always something else in his mind, you could tell. When he was young he used to read everything he could lay his hands on. The old place – his parents' place – had a lot of books. Someone said they brought them out from Ireland with them, but I don't really believe that. How would they when they couldn't read! The only one I can remember now was 'The Count of Monte Cristo'. Anyway, the books were there, and Tim read every one. Whether it was the books or not, Tim was more of a thinker. He got into the workers' movement, and used to speak at big rallies round here and up country, at Ararat and round there, chairing meetings of the District Labor Council to choose who was going to run for parliament and things like that. He was in the Australian Natives Association, too. He was on the Committee at Learmonth, I remember. I used to see him just before the War, dressed up in his suit and collar and tie. He did look a grand man, moustache and all. His name was in the paper from time to time. He was a wonderful speaker. He had certificates on the wall for first prize for things like impromptu speaking. Someone once said to me he'd go twenty miles to hear Tim Connelly speak. For whatever reason, he didn't hit it off with his mother. She used to kick him out, and he'd go to some place on his own, but he came back home after she died. He bought one or two blocks in his own name, and he seemed to have quite a bit of money one way or another, though he used to give it away when he shouldn't have, to people like my brother, Patsy, who was always asking him for a hand-out. Tim had his own home over the last years of his life. He died in St. John of God's in Ballarat.

There was always another one coming along in that family. You could count on it! Michael came after Tim. He was known as Mick. He used to go up to the Mallee chasing work, and he hurt his back lumping bags of wheat, which you had to do in those days. He was no good after that, then he got sick and died in the Base Hospital in Ballarat. He was only thirty-four, and a fine stamp of a man. Not much of a life, really, when you think about it.

Tim Connelly in A.N.A outfit, 1912

My Uncle Dick, now he was a character. He was the next. Not like the others at all. He used to call Pat, his brother, 'George.' He was always joking, especially when he'd had a few drinks. He'd come home from the pub late at night, and come in, crashing around and making a lot of noise and calling out, 'George, where are you, George, you old so-and-so?' He was closer to his brother, Tim, than any of the others. He and Tim used to go spud-digging round the district for twopence a bag! Later, Dick worked at Creelman's big place up the road. Richard Thomas was his full name. He married a Protestant girl, Lily Sadler, when he was in his mid-'forties and she was still in her 'twenties. They met on the train coming up from Melbourne. It was 1917 and Dick had just joined up. He was in uniform, and under the weather. She must have been carried away by the uniform. They only had six years together, but there were three young ones, Kathleen, Vincent, and Richard, who were christened Catholic. Uncle Dick was drunk when he went down to register Richard, and he named him Richard James Mannix, after the Archbishop! No sooner were he and Lil married than he went off to the war. Forty-something years of age! I wonder they took him, but by then the recruiting had fallen away and they were getting a bit desperate. Anyway, to finish the story, he never saw any action. He got sick over there and they sent him home with pneumonia. He was never up to much from then on and died in the Repat. Hospital in Heidelberg a few years after the war ended. They brought him back to Learmonth to bury him. There's a twist in the tale, actually. A couple of years after Dick died, Lil somehow or other managed to have another baby. Jack was his name – Jack Connelly. I don't know what happened to him. Nobody seems to know. Lil used to send the first three up to stay with Maggie, who was her sister-in-law, though it's hard to think of them like that, with the difference in their ages. After the baby was born, Lil wrote to Maggie and asked if she could come up to see her, with the baby. Maggie wrote back and said she was welcome, but not the baby. She wouldn't have another man's baby in the house. She was very proper was Maggie. Prim and proper.

Well, to go on. There were two girls to finish with, Mary Ann and Catherine. Mary Ann was crippled up and died of pneumonia in the end. Only two and a half. She used to spend all the time in a little rocking chair. About the only time she ever got out of that rocking chair was when she'd hobble over to rock the cradle when the next baby, Catherine, came along and was crying.

Catherine was the last and got terribly spoiled. She was married young, had six children, and was dead at thirty. Died about the same time as our mother. Her husband was Jim Hannabry, as if there wasn't enough Jims in the family already, but Jim Hannabry wasn't much good and cleared out. None of them ever saw him again, and I was interested to see that when they buried Catherine, she was buried under the name, Connelly, not Hannabry. When their mother died, and with their father nowhere to be seen, the younger children went to be reared by their Aunty Kate on the Curran side. She was my mother, Cecilia's, sister. I think I've got the six children off right. There was Maggie first. She married Pat Ryan and went to Waubra to set up home. Mary was next. She married Bill McMahon. Then there was Edward - Ted, they called him - who never married, but he was a bonzer bloke. He wouldn't hurt a fly, though he used to spend too much money on the horses. After that came Alice, who married a McIntosh and went to Ballarat to live, then Kathleen, who was quite a thing. She married this bloke who was well off, and lived in a big mansion at Randwick in Sydney. They were all set for an overseas trip, and had their bags packed, when she took a stroke and dropped dead at the Randwick races. The last was Jack, but I can't say I know anything about him at all.

* * *

Seeing I've just mentioned Aunty Kate, I'd better say a word about the Currans, my mother's family. The Connellys and the Currans came together when my father, William Connelly, married Cecilia Curran in 1891. Her father, Bernard and his brother, Daniel, came to Australia, from County Donegal. Daniel married Susan Patton and Bernard married Bridget Connellan. I've got a lot written down about the Daniel Curran side of the family, including all the cousins. But I won't put it in here. It would make it too complicated. Except for one strange thing. The two brothers, Daniel and Bernard Curran died on the same day in 1912, Bernard in Ballarat and Daniel in Dorrigo, a thousand miles apart!

My mother's family didn't stay fixed in one place like the Connellys did at Weatherboard. They began at Buninyong. That's where Cecilia was born, in 1866. They were at Bungaree and Warrenheip after that. There were four or five more children after Cecilia. The others were Thomas, Annie, John, Bernard and Catherine. The last two were twins, but young Bernard died soon after he was born. The one who became important to us was Catherine. She was always just 'Aunty Kate' to us, and it was to her place that I used to go whenever I could, and it was Aunty Kate who brought up my little brother and sister, John and Catherine, after my mother died. She looked after those six little ones of Cath Hannabry's as well, remember. Aunty Kate never married. She moved to Waubra eventually and died there in 1950, in her mid-seventies. The Connelly family owe her a lot. The old folk, Bernard and Bridget, lived on till a good age. He died in 1911 and she in 1922. They're both buried in the cemetery at Learmonth, like the Connellys.

The main Connelly headstone in Learmonth cemetery. The founders of the family, James and Catherine are buried here. The other names are of their children, Michael, Catherine (who married Jim Hannabry (hence 'Catherine H'), Mary Anne, William and his wife Cecilia, James ('Jim'), and Bernard ('Ben'). Ben is not here; he is buried in France

CHAPTER 6

To get back to the Connellys. In case you've got confused, it was my grandfather and grandmother, James and Catherine Connelly, who started the family here in Australia. Their oldest child, William, married Cecilia Curran, and they had eight children, and now I'll tell you about each of them in turn.

I'm the oldest child of that marriage, William Francis, born in 1892. I don't know where they got the 'Francis' from. Anyway, I'm mostly called Will. I first saw the light of day at Miners Rest, which is in closer to Ballarat from Learmonth. My parents rented a place there for a few years, before they came back to Learmonth. We children all went to the Weatherboard school, down the hill, near the lake. I never became learned, as they say, but I reckon I've got a good head on my shoulders. I was strong enough and worked on farms round about, wherever I could get a job, when I finished with school. I even went up Cowra way, in New South Wales, for a while. All the work was done with horses in those days – ploughing and harrowing, sowing and harvesting, clearing, and so on. Big teams often, and I used to handle all that pretty easily. I could run very fast and used to win some of the local races. Foot-running was a big thing in my day. I'd dream of becoming famous as a runner, and there was talk about me going up to Melbourne to be trained properly, but I never had a chance, with my background and no support. It all just faded away.

My father and mother died within a year of each other when I was seventeen or so. It didn't mean much to me at the time. I'd been staying over with the Currans more than at home for quite a while. Then the war started in 1914. They took only volunteers to go overseas, but it didn't appeal much to me, and I stayed away from it. For a while, at any rate. The next year the Gallipoli campaign began, and after that they stepped up the pressure about recruiting. There was a lot of advertising. People were getting hard on people like me about joining up and it was not easy to resist. In April – just after the Gallipoli landing, actually – I went to a social in Weatherboard for the Belgian Relief Fund and my sister, Annie, sang that song:

> *There is a land where, floating free,*
> *From mountain-top to girdling sea,*
> *A proud flag waves exultingly;*
> *And Freedom's sons the banner bear,*
> *No shackled slave can breathe the air,*
> *Fairest of Britain's daughters fair — Australia.*

It was things like that made it hard for me. The final thing was that my young brother, Jim, enlisted, here at Learmonth, and as I was the oldest in the family, I was the one who signed the permission papers. A couple of weeks later I followed suit.

There were no worries about the physical – I was five foot eight, eleven stone, light brown hair, and green eyes. That's what they wrote down. We did our preliminary training at Broadmeadows, just out of Melbourne, and after that we shipped over to Egypt on the 'Nestor'. The idea was that we were on standby for Gallipoli, but the campaign ended there before we had a chance for that, and we were sent on from Alexandria over to Marseilles in France, then by train to our position on the Somme. I was recruited into the 14th Battalion. They needed reinforcements because of the losses at Gallipoli. You might have heard of the 14th Battalion. We were famous because of Captain Albert Jacka who won the VC as well as the MC and Bar, and who was the greatest soldier and natural bushman I've ever known. They called us 'Jacka's Mob'.

I don't want to say much about the Western Front, except to tell you what happened to me. I was wounded in the foot a few months after we went into action. They put me in the Field Hospital to start with, and I was two months away from the unit. That's when I learnt some French - 'Voulez-vous promenader avec moi, Ma'amselle?' we'd say to the young ladies. That was late in 1916, and five months later came the big show at Bullecourt in April, 1917. It was part of our assault on the Hindenburg Line, as they called it. We'd had six weeks behind the lines, training for it, so most of the boys were wanting to get it over and done with. They ordered the attack for the tenth of April, and we were up most of the night, in position at 2.30 for the 4.30 kick-off. Shocking nights they were, perishing cold, sleet, snow on the ground. We were going to have tank support, just about the first time that had happened, but the tanks didn't show, and the light started to break, so it was called off until the next morning. Were we exhausted by then, even before we went into it! And we thought the Germans had seen us and would be ready for us.

The attack the next day was a disaster. The tanks were useless, getting lost in the fog or breaking down. They were supposed to knock down the wire, but not one tank reached the wire and we had to cut through it ourselves, getting fire from both flanks. Some of the men got through to the second line of trenches, and my squad of bomb-throwers followed them, but we got cut off there without any cover. All our grenades were gone; we lost connection to base command; there was nothing we could do. They took us all prisoner. I heard the Australian Army lost more men, killed, wounded, and captured, that day than any other single day of the war. We were taken to Limburg prisoner-of-war camp, which was the biggest one, and the conditions there were as good as we could have expected, except for the times they gave us thistle soup! Those of us who'd come off farms were taken out, often for months at a time, to work on farms, sometimes hundreds of miles away. I was working on an island in the Baltic Sea at one time. When the war ended and they let us out , we went over to London for a month or two, including Christmas, until they managed to get us home on the 'Ascanius'. I picked up my war gratuity, went back to Learmonth, and spent it.

*   *   *

My brother Jim, the one who joined up just before I did, eighteen years of age, went into a Trench Mortar Battery as a gunner, and went to France. He was wounded soon after he went into action and was sent over to England for treatment. The next year, 1917, he was wounded again. It was more serious this time, with bad injuries to his left leg and foot. He was in hospital in England for seven months before he could get back to the front. There was no luck for Jim at all. Six weeks later he got a really bad one when a shell exploded alongside him. Back in England again, they took his leg off this time, at the top of the thigh. He came home on the 'Marathon' in April, 1919, and was discharged. He went back to Weatherboard, to the old place, which belonged to Uncle Pat and Aunt Maggie by this time, and lived with them. He used to joke about his one leg and his crutches. He'd get his cousin, Mary Hannabry, to clean his boot and give her sixpence for it. She was a favourite of his. I suppose Jim was living on some sort of war pension. But he was never any good again, and the doctors eventually sent him to Heidelberg, where he died, only twenty-six, in 1923.

* * *

Ben was the third one to go to the war. He was only sixteen, but he put his age up and they weren't asking too many questions at that stage. He still had to get someone from the family to sign his papers, though. Uncle Pat and Aunt Maggie wouldn't sign them, and nor would Uncle Tim. But the cunning beggar went over to the Currans and got old Grandma Curran to sign them. Did that cause a row! Uncle Tim, especially, would never speak to the Currans after that, with what happened to Ben and all. Bernard Michael was his full name. He went in three months after us other two, and six months later he was in action. Sixteen! They put him in an Infantry Battalion, the

24th. He was evacuated to England twice during the two years he was in the line. The first time he was treated for some sort of medical condition, and the second time he was gassed. He must have taken a fair whiff if they had to send him away like that. Anyhow, he came back to his unit in September, 1918, just when the Germans were throwing everything at what they called the Spring Offensive. His mob survived that all right and they'd cracked the Hindenburg Line and started to drive the Germans back. The final breakthrough came on the fifth of October when they took the village of Montbrehain. It was the beginning of the end for the Germans, but there was a heavy cost. 115 Australians were killed in action that day, including Ben. It was actually the last day Australian troops were in action. That night they were relieved from duty - the Americans were moving in by then – and the war ended a few weeks later. Nineteen, Ben was, after three years of war, and killed on what would have been his last day! They buried him at Ramiecourt, which was close by, but later on, years after the war, they reburied him in the Tincourt New British Cemetery, alongside a lot of other Australians. His gratuity was paid to his little sister, Catherine.

CHAPTER 7

I've gone out of order there, to put the three of us who went to the war together. The second in the family, after me, was Annie. Ann Margaret to give her her full name. Like me, she spent a lot of her time over at the Currans. There was a fellow called Bill Gallagher, who used to drive the baker's cart. He'd call at Currans' amongst the other places, and that's where he met Annie. They got married and went to Waubra to live. That's where Bill came from.

The third was another Cecilia. Cecilia Margaret this time, Cissie, as everybody called her. Everybody used to like Cissie, but she did some funny things just the same. The brothers and I who went to the war arranged that our pay would be sent to her while we were away, but she started to spend it, so when we got home, there wasn't a lot left. I got a fair bit of mine, but my brother Jim got nothing at all. After all that, Cissie went and married an old fellow called Scotty McCrossan. She used to say, 'You won't laugh at the old man I've married, will you?' They lived down in Melbourne. I remember she came up to Weatherboard once, sick, with a big lump. Uncle Pat drove her down to the doctor in Learmonth, who told her it could be cured and gave her a letter to a specialist in Melbourne. But she wouldn't go. The next thing we heard was she'd been scrubbing the floor or something and the thing burst and killed her. That was not long after the war ended. She was still in her 'twenties.

The next in the line were the two who went to the war with me, Jim and Ben, that I've already told you of. Then came Patsy. Patsy was the one always kicking over the traces. You could understand it, him being only a kid of seven or eight when his mother and father died, and spending a lot of time living with the Currans. He used to sponge off different ones. He'd come round and say, 'Got any sugar?' He was always getting something out of his Uncle Tim. Tim gave him 300 quid, once, I think it was. Patsy hung around Weatherboard, working here and there, but he was always hankering to get away. He's a shiftless one, that one.

John was after that. Number seven. Johnnie's a good boy, but a bit different, as they say. Aunty Kate Curran was the one who reared him. She sent him to school all right, at Weatherboard, and he's clever enough, but he's no good for work. He likes to play on a little mandolin, and he can paint as well. He uses egg yolk and things like that. He goes round visiting and talking to people. Everyone likes him.

The last one was Katie, short for Catherine. It's funny that the youngest in our family was a Catherine, just like the last generation. Katie was born in 1905, so she was only four or five when her mother and father died, and still a girl when the war ended. She went to school with Johnnie at Weatherboard, like the rest of us. It's strange the things you think of. I remember she used to fight with another girl at school. This other girl, Lizzie McIntyre, would call out, 'Don't play with the Irish Connellys, don't play with the Irish Connellys!' Seems funny that people would think of us as Irish when the family had been out here for fifty years! Katie got hydatids from one of the dogs and had to have an operation. She's never looked well after that. She and Johnnie are pretty close, seeing how they both went over to Currans to live and went to school together. It couldn't have been much fun for those little ones.

Children at Weatherboard School, about 1921. My father's youngest sister, Kate is front right (probably). My father and others in his family attended here

That's the story of the Connellys as far as I want to go. None of us in the family was really close to any of the others. Most people would say that it was because our mother and our father both died young, but it was more than that. We didn't get much of an example. My dad was a bit of a waster. If he got any money it went on the horses. He didn't last long after my mother died. He fell into the water over at Lake Burrumbeet and got a chill. It was that that finished him off.

I'll finish up now. It will be up to someone else to continue the story and make their judgements on us. As for me, I'll end up by saying that after I'd hung around Learmonth for three or four years - after I got back from the war, that is – I met up with a young woman fairly fresh out from England, and, though, if you knew her, you'd probably say it was an unlikely thing to happen, we decided to get married. That's a complicated story, and I can't go into it now.

PART 2. ROSE

CHAPTER 1

THOMAS HAZARD

My name is Thomas Hazard.

It's an old name, Hazard. I've heard it said the Hazards were originally from eastern France, close to the Swiss border. They were there at the time of the Norman Conquest and later on some of the Hazards took part in the Crusades.

I can't be sure about that, and even if it were true, it doesn't have much bearing on us today. I'm told there were Hazards with the Flemish weavers who came over to England in the late Middle Ages. Then again, they say there were Hazards amongst the French Huguenots who fled from France in the 1680s under persecution from the Catholic regime. One of those Hazards was put to death when he returned to France. I think the Flemish weavers origin is more likely. For one thing, the Hazards I've known are strong in their faith, but not the sort to want to die for it, like some of the Huguenots did.

The first I can pick up of our family line were in Nottingham. There are records of Hazards in Nottinghamshire in the early sixteenth century. The name there seems to have been Hassard to begin with. There was a Philip Hassard who had a son, John, who was the first to be known as Hazard, and he, in turn, had a son, William. This William produced a son, Thomas, who married Margarit Pawmer in 1589, but he went off to Rhode

Island in the American colonies. The Hazards there became famous as early settlers and leaders in public affairs. One of them is revered as one of the founding fathers of Newport, Rhode Island. These Hazards are undoubtedly our Hazards, but I can't connect them in a direct line.

The first Hazard I can definitely trace our ancestry back to was from Wilford in Nottinghamshire. Wilford is a few miles from Nottingham itself, and Nottingham was well-known in the weaving trade. That's further support for the Flemish origins.

The parish records in Wilford show there was a Robert Hazard buried there in 1658 or 1659. It's hard to tell from the writing which year it was. In 1666 (the year London was burning down, if I remember correctly), a woman referred to as 'Widow Hazard' was buried at Wilford, and it's safe to assume she was Robert's widow.

This is now the Year of our Lord 1887 - two hundred and twenty years later, and I can trace my line of descent through seven generations from Robert and 'Widow' Hazard to myself. In the early years, the details are rather flimsy, and I have only some of the names that flowed into our line of descent from the marriages that took place over that time. But I will stick to the Hazard lineage, and tell you what I can.

*　*　*

I can't vouch for everything about those early days. I'm depending on the parish records at Wilford, and they don't show such things as who the parents were. And after a generation or two there were several lines of Hazards living (and dying!) there. But I've spent a lot of time on this and I think I've got it right.

It seems that Robert and 'Widow' Hazard had a son, William. (I'll call him William the First for reasons you'll soon understand). He married a wife, Elizabeth, and they had many children, although only three survived. The three who survived were John, George, and William. The other five died at birth or in infancy. They were Humphrey, Robert, and Joseph, Benjamin, and Anne. The latter three were triplets. It's sad to think of those lost little ones and the grief their parents must have suffered. I also reflect on the names of those who died, some of them now sounding so foreign in the light of the family's ongoing history.

One of those boys who survived, William (William the Second), married a wife with the Christian name of Valentine, and it was they who carried on our particular family line. I know quite a bit about these two, but I'd like to know more - what sort of people they were and how they lived out their lives, but, alas, this sort of knowledge has been lost for ever.

This William the Second died in 1718, and his widow, Valentine, was married again five years later to a Phillip ffolton or Felton, and lived, remarkably, until 1753. She must been a good age, especially for those times. Before her first husband, William Hazard's, death, Valentine bore him eight children. They were, in order, Elizabeth, Anne, who married Thomas Radford, Sarah and William who were twins, John who died in infancy, a second John, George, and Dorothy, who was born after her father's death, but who only lived a short while. It's the second John we're interested in, because it was he who carried on the line.

This John Hazard was born in 1713, and lived to be almost eighty. In his lifetime, he saw the American colonies gain their independence, the start of the French Revolution, and the first white settlement in Australia. He also lived to see his grandchildren, which was often not the case in the eighteenth century. His wife, Mary, was also quite a long-liver. She died at sixty-nine, eight years before her husband. John and Mary had two children, William (the third William in four generations!) and Charles, though I've altogether lost track of Charles.

This William Hazard (William the Third) was a farmer. That's the first mention I have of an occupation in the known family tree, and I'm very interested to see it there. The Hazards haven't been known as farmers in recent generations. The law is their line. William married twice, first to Hannah Rossell from Draycott, which is close by, just the other side of Nottingham. Hannah died at the age of thirty-three, but not before giving birth to my grandfather. William's second marriage was to Elizabeth Lockton. There was a son and a daughter born to William and Elizabeth. The son was Charles, though he's slipped out of sight, too. I don't know the girl's first name, although I do know she married a Mr Watson, a hatter and hosier from Newark, further away in Nottinghamshire. You could say he catered for the top end and the lower end of his customers!

That first child, my grandfather, had the same name as I have - Thomas Hazard. He left his father's farm, and became a builder and cabinet-maker, with premises in High Pavement, Nottingham. I have his business card – the earliest family personal possession I have. Thomas lived only to the age of twenty-six, but fortunately for the Hazard pedigree, he had married a wife two years earlier, Sarah Parslee, who came from Norwich. Sarah produced two children, twins, William (sorry about that!), who became my father, and Mary, who died as an infant. Their father died in the same year, 1799. It must have been a sad time for Sarah, losing her baby daughter and her husband so close together. Father and daughter lie together now in the Wilford graveyard, nestled in a fold of the River Trent. Thomas's mother, Hannah, and his grandparents, John and Mary, are close by. Not long after being widowed, Sarah was re-married to William John Livock, a widower. Sarah bore two more children, Sarah and Charlotte, but they both died young, the first aged eight and the second as an infant. My father was brought up with his mother and step-father in the Livock household. The Livocks removed from Nottingham to Harleston in Norfolk, and that's a turning-point in the history of our Hazard family.

* * *

Now we come to my father, and the introduction of the Hazards to the profession of the law. My father, William Hazard (William the Fourth), entered that noble profession and became an attorney-at-law. As a youth, he was quite famous, he used to tell me, for crossing the Trent on the ice one January day. That was back in the days when Wilford was famous for its cherry-eating festival. William married his cousin, Elizabeth Parslee, his mother's brother's daughter. The marriage was at St. Nicholas' in Great Yarmouth, the great fishing port on the Norfolk coast, which rejoices, I understand, in being the largest parish church in England. St Nicholas is the patron saint of fishermen! If ever there was Huguenot blood in the Hazards, they were solidly 'Church' by now!

William, my father, was in practice in Harleston, but developed many other interests there. He was Clerk to the Magistrates and agent for Gurney's Bank, a Norwich commercial house founded by the Gurneys, the famous family of Quakers, who had an unshakeable reputation for integrity. In fact our whole family lived upstairs in the Gurney's Bank building in Harleston, in Old Market Place. We five children were all born in Harleston. There was a sixth child, actually, born twelve months before me, a boy, never given a name, and who died at the age of ten weeks. My mother, to my deep anguish, died young, at thirty-five, when I was five years old, and is buried in Redenhall Churchyard, the parish church of Harleston. My father now lies there with her. Everyone says my mother was a beautiful soul. Her tombstone refers to her as "the most affectionate, exemplary, and beloved wife of William Hazard."

Perhaps I could give you a picture of our household in the year, 1851, mid-century, and the year of the Great Exhibition at Crystal Palace. My mother had been gone for many years by then. My father, who was born at the turn of the century, was fifty-one years old, my brother, William Martin, twenty-two, myself, Thomas, twenty years old, my sister, Elizabeth, nineteen, and the baby of the family, Anne, seventeen. Anne was a mere baby when our mother died. To complete the household, we had a cook, a housemaid, and an under-housemaid. My brother was also an attorney-at-law, in my father's practice. I was also in the firm, articled to my father at that stage, while Elizabeth and Anne were at home. My father had a business partner, John Jeffs, for a few years, until my brother turned twenty-one, when he was admitted as a partner. The practice was then known as 'Hazard and Son'.

You probably noticed there that I mentioned only four of the five children. The one I left out was the oldest, actually – my brother Charles, born in 1826. By 1851, he had left home and was employed at Somerset House in London as a clerk in the Registry of Births, Deaths, and Marriages. Charles was born deaf and dumb, although that didn't prevent him from leading an active life. In London he was a Committee-member of the Society for the Propagation of the Gospel's outreach to the Deaf and Dumb. Part of that work was to organise a Christmas Dinner to which all the deaf and dumb people in London were invited. He was also a leading figure in the Association in Aid of the Deaf and Dumb. At their Annual General Meeting in 1868 he presented an address, read by another person. He was also on the Committee of Management of the Aged and Infirm Deaf and Dumb Society, whose main work was to provide pensions for needy individuals. His greatest joy was to go walking on the Continent - in Germany and Switzerland - where he and some friends would go in summer. When my wife and I moved to London later on, Charles lived with us at our place in Stoke

Newington. In 1872, Charles went abroad again, and died, apparently of a heart attack, in Berlin. He was forty-six.

When my father died in 1856, my brother, William Martin (I'll continue to call him that in order to distinguish him from the other Williams), as oldest son and partner to my father, took over the practice. He maintained the agency for Gurney's and remained as Clerk to the Magistrates. He was also the representative of several different insurance companies. His wealth increased and he invested in things like the Greater Western Railway. Within a year or two, he had purchased and moved into the fine estate of Caltofts, easily the grandest house in the town, which stands in a prime position at the head of Broad Street. Later, he bought the Lordship of the Manor of Harleston, so was by name as well as by common respect 'the Lord of the Manor'. He had married three years earlier, very soon after our father's death. His wife was Mary Daniel, the daughter of the Reverend John Daniel, who had been the Vicar of Weybread in Suffolk, just over the Waveney, the county boundary. My brother was a conscientious and vigorous churchman. He excised part of the Caltofts property as a gift for the building of a new church and gave a large sum towards its construction. He continued as an active churchman in the new St John the Baptist Church until his death. He paid Mrs Munnings, the mother of the famous artist, fifteen pounds a year to play the organ. My brother died in 1883, four years ago, at the age of fifty-four. There are now memorial windows to him in both our own church here in Harleston and in the parish church, St. Mary's, Redenhall, where he was Churchwarden. He and Mary had no family.

St John the Baptist's Harleston, adjoining Caltofts and built on land given by William Martin Hazard in 1871. Several of the memorial windows are to members of the Hazard family

I've spoken of the first two in the family, Charles and William Martin. I came next, but I'll hold fire about myself for a little and turn next to my sisters. Both Elizabeth and Anne did exquisite work with their crochet and knitting. We still have their pattern books, dated from 1847, many of them laboriously copied out by hand in small notebooks. Elizabeth, who was always known as Lizzie, married Gerard Barton from Stoughton in Essex. They had twelve children, and one of them, the oldest, Bernard, re-enters our story a little later. Anne married into the well-known Candler family, who also link back into the family in a later generation. Anne's husband, John Candler, was the doctor in Harleston for decades. He was a widower, having been previously married to a Miss Robinson. There were two children of the first marriage, Bessie and Willie. Willie became a doctor, like his father. They practised together in Harleston until Willie died, pre-deceasing his father. The family lived in the surgery, which they named 'Candler's', in the centre of Harleston.

*   *   *

Finally, I come back to myself. I was born in 1830, on St. Thomas's Day, the twenty-first of December, but whether I was named in honour of the saint or of my grandfather, I know not. I will shortly be fifty-seven years old, and have been a widower these last twenty-seven years. You know already that I am the third son of my parents, William and Elizabeth, not allowing for my next-older brother who died in infancy. I followed my father into the law, but while my brother, William Martin, joined our father in practice in Harleston, I was sent to London – to Lincoln's Inn - to pursue the firm's interests there. I had a wonderful but tragic marriage. In 1856 my beloved Jane and I were married at St Clement's in Ipswich, Jane's native town. It was barely two months before my father's death. Jane's parents – Richard and Mary Ann Porter - were very well-known in Ipswich. Richard Porter was a solicitor and Treasurer to the town of Ipswich. We returned to London and had four years of great happiness. Three children were born – William Henry, Anna Mary, and Elizabeth Jane. Then my wife began to sicken. In October of 1860, at Hastings, where she had gone in an endeavour to recapture her health, my dear wife was taken from me. In the midst of my grief, little Elizabeth Jane died also, five months later. At the age of thirty, I found myself a widower, at the head of a small family, William Henry, then three, and Anna Mary, two.

We remained in London for over twenty years - in Islington, Grove West, and Kidbrooke - until the death of my brother, William Martin, four years ago, when I returned to Harleston to take his place in the firm, which by then was 'Hazard and Pratt', Thomas Pratt having not long before become a partner. Two years later, I took up residence in my brother's former home, Caltofts. Mary, his widow, moved to a house in Broad Street, Earsham, not far away. That was just twelve months ago. My two children are now in their late 'twenties, about to step out into the fullness of their own lives. Indeed, my son, William Henry, is setting out on his own life in the law, having recently joined me in my practice here in Harleston. Meanwhile I look forward to my continued service to the people of this town and to length of years in this peaceful place.

William Henry and Anna Mary Hazard. Aged nearly 4 and 2 ½ Photo taken on glass at Mr Olley's house, 22 June, 1861. William Henry Olley was a pioneering London photographer

William Henry Hazard

Anna Mary Hazard

CHAPTER 2

JOYCE WINIFRED HAZARD

Time has moved us on. It is my task to take up my grandfather's story. It is a sorrowful task, for I have to tell of the shattering of that peace my grandfather, Thomas Hazard, spoke of, and of the coming of war, the death of those closest to my heart, the breaking up of my family, and their scattering to the four winds.

I am Joyce, second daughter and fifth child of William Henry Hazard. My father was one of the two surviving children of Thomas Hazard, as you would have read. I shall follow his pattern and go methodically through the family, one by one, beginning with my grandfather himself.

He concluded his account in 1887, but, sadly, died three years later, when he was sixty. His hope of a long and peaceful life in Caltofts was not granted. His two children were still single, so there were no grandchildren to cheer his last years. My father and mother were married two years after his death and my Aunt Anna several years later again. Thomas Hazard is buried in Redenhall churchyard, together with so many others of my family.

Without their mother, William Henry and Anna were brought up by a housekeeper, though they spent much of the time with their Porter grandparents in Ipswich. I don't think they enjoyed that very much. The old folk were rigid to the point of stuffiness.

Redenhall St Mary, three kilometres from Harleston. The parish church. A fifteenth century building with Victorian remodelling. The bells rang out to warn of the approaching Armada in 1588

It was not much of a childhood for them, especially as their father, Thomas, withdrew into himself as time went on.

Perhaps I could write of Aunt Anna before I come to my father. The two of them were never very close in adult life, actually. Aunt Anna was a very kind person. She always had a soft spot for me, and I for her. She lived a genteel life as a single lady until her late 'thirties, much of the time with her aunt Mary Hazard, who was widowed, and lived in Earsham. They lived as refined ladies, 'living on their own means' as it used to be put. Then Bernard Barton asked her to marry him. He was a sweet old man, as I remember him. Aunt Anna's aunt, Lizzie Hazard, had married Gerard Barton, and Bernard was their son. So it was a case of the marriage of two cousins. Bernard was a little older than Anna. Uncle Bernard, as he became to me, was a teacher, then was ordained, and eventually went off to Canada to be Chaplain to a very peculiar settlement in Manitoba, miles from anywhere. It was called Cannington Manor at a place with a very queer name, Assiniboia. It was a kind of agricultural college for the sons of wealthy British settlers, although it never really got going and failed altogether after a time. Uncle Bernard asked Aunt Anna to go out there and marry him, and she accepted. The wedding was in Winnipeg in August, 1862. They eventually returned to England and lived in London, where Bernard became a parish vicar, before settling near Harleston. He rode a sit-up-and-beg bicycle, and looked rather like Bernard Shaw. He was very eccentric. He wore old-fashioned clothes, and to see him on his bicycle wearing his caped overcoat was amusing to say the least. We used to laugh at him, I'm afraid to say. Anna was much corseted and wore black silk, very prim indeed. She seemed to live in a past age, and thought that we children were hopelessly ill-behaved. They were a very devoted couple, however. Bernard always called Anna his 'Lady-Love'. I have two lovely photos of Bernard and Anna, each holding closely to the other. Aunt Anna and I have kept up with each other, even though we're now a world apart. I'll add one more thing about Bernard and Aunt Anna. It is through the Bartons that we have a connection with the royal family, and I mention this in jest through and through! George V's daughter, Princess Mary (the Princess Royal) married Viscount Lascelles. His half-brother – William Lascelles, son of Lord Harewood – married Madge Barton (her actual name was Madeline Barton), sister of Bernard Barton, husband of Anna, who was the sister of my father, William Henry Hazard!

I adored my father, though I was never quite sure what he thought of me. And I always felt a kind of sadness for him. He was known as 'Henry', but he retained a sense of formality, even to us children, for instance signing his letters to us with his full name. When his father, Thomas Hazard, died, he succeeded to the partnership in Hazard and Pratt in Harleston. My father had grown up in London while his father was attending to the family's concerns there at the office in Old Jewry. Then he studied Law, and graduated from London University with Honours in 1880, when he was twenty-three. It was now his turn to run the London end of affairs, and he did this for ten years until he came to Harleston to become the senior partner after his father's death in 1890. He was then in his mid-thirties and single, but that was about to change. He fell in love with a young woman, scarcely more than a girl. They met when she came to Norfolk recovering from an illness. Her name was Marguerite Tooth, always called Margot, and she was to become my mother.

Anna Mary Barton, sister of William Henry Hazard

Bernard and Anna Mary Barton, Cambridge

CHAPTER 3

I have to go back in time now to explain about the Tooths, and this will take some time. The younger generation seem to be quite as interested in the Tooth side of the family as they are in the Hazards. There is as much Tooth blood flowing in my veins as Hazard blood, I suppose, and I felt much closer to my mother than my father. Yet I've always felt myself a Hazard rather than a Tooth. Someone in the family once said that the Hazards were noble-minded while the Tooths were intellectual. That's much too simple, of course, though there's more than a grain of truth in it. The women amongst the Tooths were held to be very beautiful, though not perhaps not so much in my generation, I'm afraid! The men in the Tooth family are mostly slim and have a distinctive strong and long face. But there is more to the comparison than that. I can't help feeling the overwhelming sense of gloom that has hung over the Hazards in recent years, while the Tooths have brought lightness and laughter into the family, despite also having known their sadnesses.

There's been so much written about the Tooths I'll be as brief as I can. The Tooths were a well-known family from Cranbrook in Kent, but much more famous in Australia. The first Tooth I know about was John Tooth who married a wife called Sarah in 1767. They had six children, Edwin, Sarah, Susannah, William Butler, Robert, and John. William Butler Tooth married Catherine Butler – a cousin, I presume. Catherine produced twelve children. Two of them are important for our story. The third one of the twelve was Robert and the sixth was John.

Robert was my great-grandfather and John my great-great-uncle.

John, who married Elizabeth Newnham, was the first Tooth to come to Australia. He went into business as a merchant and commission agent in Sydney, before starting up a brewery at Blackwattle Creek in 1835 in partnership with his brother-in-law, Charles Newnham. The Tooths were acute businessmen and used to moving in moneyed circles in both England and Australia. As well as the brewery, John Tooth also accumulated large property holdings. The brewery went through hard times in its first years because of the Depression that occurred in the early 'forties, and three of his nephews, sons of his brother Robert, came out from Cranbrook to help the business out of its difficulties. They were Robert, Edwin, and Frederick Tooth. The brewery eventually became the greatest in the land, and the three brothers went on to become amongst the wealthiest and most powerful men in the colonies.

Back in England, Robert Tooth became an important and wealthy man. I'll call him Robert (Snr) to distinguish him from Robert Tooth (Jnr), his son, my grandfather. Robert Tooth (Snr) was a hat manufacturer, but diversified into brewing. He was so wealthy that he is said to have given each of his eight sons five thousand pounds when they turned twenty-one. That was an enormous sum. In the 1860s he had invested heavily in the merchant house, Overend and Gurney, who themselves were financially interwoven with the finance house, London and Colonial. In 1866, both of these institutions collapsed and Robert lost all his money. Six months later he was dead. The cause of death was 'urea on the brain', which is associated with mercury poisoning. Mercury was then used in making hats, and it seems very likely that his early life as a hat-maker eventually caused his death. His widow, Fanny, died intestate five years later.

The Tooths were given to having large families. Robert Tooth (Snr) married twice. His first wife was Mary Anne Reader. She bore him eleven children, one of whom died in infancy. I'll make a list of them:

> Robert (1821-1893). My grandfather. Married first Marcia Lisle Forster, and secondly Elizabeth Mansfield.
>
> Edwin (1822-1858). Married Sarah Lucas.
>
> Alfred (born 1824). Married Adelaide Lainson.
>
> Frederick (1827-1893). Married first Jane Jackson, then Susan Frances Gosling, and thirdly Fanny Peach.
>
> John Sidney (1828-1829).
>
> Charles (1831-1894). Later the Reverend Charles. Married Elizabeth Tabberer, and later Louisa Janette Anne Richards.
>
> Henry (born 1833). Married Ann Edwards.

William Augustus (1834-1912+). Later the Reverend William. Married Eliza Petar.

Mary Anne (born 1837). Married the Reverend Christopher Nevile.

Arthur (1839-1931). Later the Reverend Arthur (Father Tooth).

Eliza Jane (born 1841).Married Marmaduke Coghill Cramer Roberts

After Anne's death, Robert Tooth (Snr) married his cousin, Fanny Tooth, who had four children:

Fanny Blanche (born 1848). Married John Edward Fincham.

Annie Maud (1850-1911). Married Compton Norman.

Roberta Catherine Ann (1852-1900). Married Ernest Cotterill.

Gertrude Gower (born 1856). Married George Robins.

Robert was twenty-two when his first child was born, and fifty-seven when his last child was born, or to put things in a different way, my grandfather, Robert (Jnr) had a sister thirty-five years younger than he was!

I've got a family tree of the Tooths and it covers the whole of my kitchen table when I spread it out. I can't possibly tell you all about those fourteen children here, except to say that while three of the older ones, Robert (Jnr), Edwin and Frederick were making their fortune in New South Wales, three of the younger ones sought a different treasure by becoming clergymen. All three, extraordinarily, were ordained in the same year, 1864. One of them, William, spent twenty years as the Chaplain of the Warren Farm Schools at Brighton, an industrial training school for the children of paupers. Another, Charles, went to Italy and is remembered as the founder of St. Mark's Church in Florence. The third deserves more space!

This third one was Arthur Tooth, or Father Tooth, as he will be known for all time. As a young man, after graduating in Science from Cambridge, he took his five thousand pounds and travelled round the globe, visiting Australia twice. On one occasion, in outback Queensland, he was lost in the bush and managed to find his own way back to safety. He was a superb rider and a crack shot. While in Australia Arthur had another saving experience in that he was converted to a life-long Christian faith. He became a Church of England priest in London, devoted to the Catholic style of worship. In the 1870s, churchmanship became a burning political issue. Members of Parliament were swept up in the Evangelical movement, and a law was passed making Catholic practices like wearing vestments and burning incense unlawful in the Church of England. They were able to do this because of the Church being an Established Church, governed by the laws of Parliament. Father Tooth refused to follow the new laws, which led to terrible trouble. Thousands of people were protesting – on both sides - in the streets outside his church, St James' in Hatcham. Hundreds of police were needed to keep order. There were dramatic scenes outside and inside the church between rival factions. At one time Father Tooth was locked out of his own church, but someone broke a window, and he got in and celebrated the Mass, as they called it. My grandfather, Robert Tooth, weighed in on behalf of his brother. "They let other people alone, and why should not they, the Ritualists, be let alone," he wrote. Father Tooth was charged with contempt of court and spent five weeks in gaol, as did four other priests, before public protests forced the government to release them. A Court of Appeal later found the proceedings against Father Tooth to have been invalid. Instead of pressing claims for damages for false imprisonment, to which he was entitled, he acted with grace and quietly resigned his charge. After that, he turned his energies to the orphanages and schools he had already established, as well as the Order of the Holy Paraclete, a sisterhood also founded by him, and which ran a home for alcoholics. All this he did chiefly by using my grandfather, his brother's, money. A huge amount has been written about Father Tooth.

Robert (Jnr), my grandfather, was the first of those three brothers who came out to Sydney to rescue their uncle's brewing business. There are dozens of different Tooth families in Australia – most of them in Queensland and New South Wales, and I keep being asked about them. But I haven't taken much interest in the descendants of the other two, Edwin and

'The Christian Martyr' Cartoon by Spy, Vanity Fair, February, 1877

Frederick. I'm going almost entirely to keep to our own family line – those of us who belong to Robert Tooth's family.

When Robert was twenty-eight, he went on a visit from Sydney to his next brother, Edwin, who by that time was living in Tasmania, where he built a fine house called 'Capricornia' at Bagdad, near Hobart. There's a very romantic story about Edwin. Once he was on board a ship coming out here to Australia and fell in love with a young lady called Sarah Lucas, who was accompanying her brother, an army officer, on his way to take up an appointment in India. Some say they were married at the Cape, some say in India, others in Sydney. (Some say that a great-aunt of Sarah's, Fanny Lucas, was the mistress of George IV; others say that she was his illegitimate daughter!).

Well, while he was staying with Edwin and Sarah at Bagdad, Robert met and married Marcia Lisle Forster, from Brighton, near Hobart. She was seventeen years old and very beautiful! Edwin's wife, Sarah, described her as having "the most lovely face I ever beheld, and her figure is equally to be admired." The wedding was at St. Mark's Church in nearby Pontville. That was in 1849. But great sadness was to follow. Marcia had a succession of children - I know of at least four - but all died at birth or before the age of eighteen months. Except for this: I have a persistent memory from my childhood of being told that one son did survive. His name was Noel and he committed suicide when still young. Perhaps someone will discover if this is true in the years to come. After suffering the loss of her little ones, Marcia herself died.

In 1871, Robert Tooth, who was then fifty years old was back in England. He was visiting his brother, Father Tooth, in Hatcham, when he saw across the street a woman he took to be the 'ghost' of his late wife, Marcia. It's a very romantic story. This woman became his second wife. She was Elizabeth Mansfield, the daughter of Joseph and Elizabeth Mansfield. Joseph Mansfield was a silversmith and jeweller from Shaftesbury in Dorset, but had just moved to Hatcham. They were married by Robert's brother, the indomitable Father Tooth, at his church, St James'. Robert's wife, Elizabeth, had an older sister, Ellen, and an older brother, Thomas, who followed his father's trade in Shaftesbury. Ellen lived until she was very old and was known as 'Big Aunty' in the family. I have heard it said that the Mansfields had a German Jewish background and that the family name was originally Mansfeldt. If there's anything in that story, Elizabeth had long been a staunch member of the Church of England. Elizabeth began a second family for Robert, all healthy this time, I'm glad to say. Five boys and three girls. My mother, Marguerite, was the first, and was born in Australia three years before the family's permanent return to England. That was at Yengarie, near Maryborough in Queensland where her father had a sugar mill and was experimenting with meat-preserving. Margot, as she was always known, could remember the little black children at Yengarie and feeding them pieces of sugar cane to stop them crying.

As well as having a share in the brewery, this Robert Tooth was one of the founders of the Twofold Bay Pastoral Association, which had huge holdings in New South Wales, including Kameruka, near Bega, which has remained in the family ever since. Later he acquired a string of squatting properties, some of them quite famous, like Jondaryan on the Darling Downs. He had his sugar mill at Yengarie, and sugar plantations as well. He was an awfully clever man, and very inventive. In 1865 he went to Germany to inspect the meat-preserving process of a man called Baron Liebig. He bought the patent, and won a prize at the Intercolonial Exhibition for his work in preserving and shipping meat to England. He was on the Board of the largest Bank in the colony, the Bank of New South Wales, and of several commercial houses like Colonial Sugar Refineries, and also a member of the Legislative Council, which was the colonial parliament at that time. As well, he did a lot for many charitable and church organisations, like Christ Church St Lawrence and St Paul's College at the new Sydney University. In 1859, he built a great house on the slopes above Sydney Harbour, and named it 'Cranbrook.' I'm telling all this so you will appreciate the magnitude of the fall, when it came. In the early 'seventies, Robert Tooth sold up many of his Australian interests and returned to London with his wife, Elizabeth, and little Margot, although he continued to travel frequently between England and the colonies. Some in the family believe he handed some of his Australian assets to his nephew, Robert, Edwin's son, the one who took the name Lucas-Tooth.

In 1883 Robert Tooth lost all that he had. I can't work out the reasons. There was a severe drought in Queensland in the early 'eighties. This was just before artesian water was discovered. And, quite separately, the sugar price fell steeply. Perhaps he over-invested in his property in Brisbane. At the time when he became insolvent, he had one major asset - a large sugar mill and brewery, the Eagle Brewery, at Bulimba on the Brisbane River. In May 1883 the liquidators sold it up. The Brisbane Courier advertised the property as having seven acres of land, a twenty-chain frontage to deep water in the Brisbane River, a manager's cottage, offices, and machinery. The advertisement was addressed to 'Capitalists, Brewers, Sugar Refiners and others'. It was, the paper said, 'one of the grandest properties ever submitted to auction in Brisbane'. It was bought by a party of local investors for £15,500, which, the liquidators announced, was sufficient to discharge all the liabilities of Robert Tooth's company – with nothing left over, presumably.

Robert had lived quite an opulent life in New South Wales, but it was more subdued after the crash. He and Elizabeth lived first in Brighton, and afterwards at The Avenue, Kew Gardens, where they were members of St. Luke's, Richmond, which was almost next door. Years later, their children had a memorial window put in for them. Finally they moved to Chaucer Road, Bedford, largely so that the children, who were still at school, could receive a better education. My grandfather died at Bedford in 1893, ten years after 'the fall'. His estate amounted to 201 pounds. Elizabeth, however, was apparently able to live in comfortable circumstances for the rest of her life, first returning to Brighton, then successively in Holland Park Avenue, Kensington South, then in Royal Crescent, Kensington. Afterwards she moved to Wellington Street, St Pancras West, and finally to Lichfield Road, Kew Gardens. The children had left home successively. At the end only her son Edwin was with her, and a servant girl. She died at Steyning in Sussex in 1917 when she was seventy-two, although I can't tell how she came to be there on the south coast.

* * *

My mother, Margot, was the oldest of the eight Tooth children, but I won't say any more about her, just now. I'll come to her later. Instead, I'll tell of her sisters and brothers.

Winnie came next after my mother. She was a darling. Everyone loved Winnie. My second name came from her (I'm Joyce Winifred), so I have a very soft spot for my Aunt Winifred. Winnie married a doctor, Clifford Barnes, but he died the year after they were married. There was talk in the family that he caught a tropical disease when he was inspecting some ships at the London docks, while others say he caught something from a patient. How sad it must have been! Winnie then gave her life to good works. She was very thin and gaunt (like a Tooth, really!) and wore long heavy tweed skirts and old-fashioned hats. She was always stately and proper - not proud, but never frivolous. Winnie was devoted to her parents' church, St Luke's. She lived nearby, in Lichfield Road, and ran the Sunday school for ages, together with another widow, Mrs Winter. I always think of a funny story I heard about Winnie. Audrey and Kit Candler, as children, lived not far from their Aunt Winnie and often visited her. They were so cold as they walked home along North Road they kept rubbing their hands together as they went, saying, "Damn and blast! Damn and blast! Damn and blast!" all the way. Aunt Winnie and Mrs Winter eventually moved in together, but, sad to tell, they had a falling out. It seemed to change Winnie's character, and she became more difficult to deal with.

Edwin was next, the first boy in the family. 'Uncle Eddie' to us. Edwin married Mabel Barnes, Clifford's sister, so making up a neat quadrilateral of Tooths and Barneses - on paper, at least, but not in life, because of Clifford dying so early. The Barneses, I might say, had money behind them. Their law firm was Collissons and Dawes. Edwin was a stockbroker, but seemed to spend most of his later life in Norfolk. He lived at Morningthorpe and later at Wortham. Mabel had nervous trouble, especially after her son, Waltheof's, birth, and had to go away for a time. Waltheof was looked after by others in the

'Aunt Winnie', second of the eight children of Robert and Elizabeth Tooth, Joyce Winifred Hazard was named after her

family, and for a long time had a nanny, Florence. Florence was once asked by Waltheof the meaning of 'purdah'. "In solution," she replied. Waltheof was their only child. Mabel had another brother called Shepperson, also a doctor, who married and went to Australia, but died shortly after. There was a daughter, Dulcie. Dulcie's mother brought her back to England, where she was cared for by Mabel, though not very well, I'm afraid. She was very unhappy. The name, Shepperson, comes from a forebear on the Barnes side, who was a notable artist many years ago. Another of Mabel's brothers, Gerald, changed his name to Buxton-Barnes, when he married into the Buxtons, a wealthy banking family. Uncle Eddie was pleasant - amiable and retiring, thin, and typically Tooth-like in appearance. Mabel, who was known as 'Minko' within the family, was very forthright, which didn't always make her very popular with the others. She would make cutting comments on what people were wearing. "You are looking very *yellow* today, Audrey," she once said to my cousin.

Next came Olive. At least, she was christened Olive, but used 'Olave' later in life. There's a village of St Olave further down the Waveney. Perhaps that's why she liked that name. Olive was very beautiful. She and Margot were regarded as the beauties of the family. Olive married Edmund Candler, which makes the second connection between my family and the Candlers. My great-aunt, Anne Hazard, had married Dr John Candler, Edmund's father. Olive's life story is rather consumed in her husband's, because he became quite famous and she went wherever he went, like Ruth and Naomi in the Bible, except that for long periods Edmund was overseas, during the war and at other times. Edmund Candler made his name when he was the Daily Mail correspondent with Colonel Younghusband's famous incursion into Tibet in 1904. He lost his hand in a battle there, but went on with the expedition. His book about the campaign, 'The Unveiling of Lhasa', is a classic, everyone says. He spent the Great War as a war correspondent in Mesopotamia, which was a great trial, personally, to him, because of his diabetes. There was no insulin then. Edmund became an expert on India and the Middle East. He was a tutor in princely families and Principal of the vast Mohindra College at Patiala for a time. He and Olive spent many years in India. He wrote a dozen books, mostly on India, but including an autobiography and some fiction as well. His books are seen now as being very advanced for their time. He was awarded a CBE. Edmund Candler became a good friend of Joseph Conrad. There are many letters between them. E.M. Forster was also a friend. Edmund and Olive retired to Hendaye on the Basque Coast of France, and ran a guest house there, though there was never much money in it. Edmund and Olive had two children, Audrey and Christopher, who was known as Kit. Audrey married Bill McGeagh, whose father was a doctor at Queens University, Belfast. Their daughter is Rachael. Audrey's brother, Kit, married Dorothy Few and lived in Johannesburg. They had no children.

In case you're getting lost, I'm Joyce Hazard, and I'm writing here about the Tooths, my mother's brothers and sisters, my uncles and aunts, that is.

Cecil was the next in the family. He suffered from TB and went on a cruise to help his recovery. On board he met his wife-to-be, Patty. She was there for her lungs as well. Patty's sister was a Dame at Eton. I remember Patty more than Cecil, because Patty used to come to Caltofts quite often when I was a child. There was one time when my mother arranged a big garden party, then fell ill. Patty Tooth and her sister, Ethel, stepped in and managed it all. Cecil and Patty lived at Hassocks in West Surrey, then at Aspley Guise, near Bedford, which became a kind of central point for many in the family. Later they lived in Harleston, on the road coming in from Needham, near Miss Saunders, who was a governess at Caltofts and very dear to me (though my sister Janet hated her). Cecil himself was sickly all his life (and he drank a little), but he did manage to play golf. His TB eventually caught up with him. There were no children.

Lawrence was known as Lonny. 'Uncle Lonny.' He was thought to be very clever, and no doubt was. He became a barrister, with rooms in Paper Building at the Temple, Kings Bench Walk. He spent some time overseas – in quite exotic places like Bangkok and Nairobi. I remember him as a serious thin man. He never married.

Wilfred struck a different note. He had his heart set on being a farmer, and went to Weybread, to the Candlers, to learn about farming. (John Candler our doctor friend, had retired by now. He and Anne moved from Harleston to Weybread House, outside the town. Everybody loved Dr Candler. When he retired in 1901, he was presented with an illuminated address and 100 pounds subscribed by the townspeople. He and Anne had six children, Bella, George, Katherine, Harry, Charlie, and Edmund, all wonderful people. I wish I had the space to say more about them here. The Candlers and the Hazards remained very close.) After being with the Candlers, Wilfred went to Canada, to British Columbia, and married out there. His wife was Florence, and they had a son, Max, who was killed in a flying accident when he was in his early twenties. After Wilfred died, Florence married again and had a daughter, Lily.

The last in the line was Harold Selwyn, or 'King,' as he was invariably known. I think it came about because, as the youngest, he was 'king of the family'. The 'Selwyn' was after Bishop George Augustus Selwyn, the great missionary Bishop of New Zealand and later of Lichfield, who was a great friend of the Tooth family. King studied law, but gave it up and went out to Assam as a tea-planter. By then he'd married his wife, Winifred Watson from Northern Ireland. They were both as thin as broomsticks! In India, King and Win sometimes stayed with Olive and Edmund Candler. They then came back to Northern Ireland. Win died, and King led a rather nomadic life after that, living with various members of the family which seems to have been a characteristic of the Tooths. He was with Audrey and Bill McGeagh at Brockdish Hall for some time. Then he went to his sister, Olive, at 'The Firs' in Pulham St Mary's. (Olive once got a letter addressed to 'The Fires,' which became a family joke!) In the end, King got cancer. When the McGeaghs moved to Hendaye, King went to live with Uncle Edwin and Aunt Mabel, and died in 1958, when he was seventy-four. He is buried in Morningthorpe churchyard, next to Edwin. He and Win had no children. King was a very likeable man, sympathetic and kind, although some of the cynics in the family, like Audrey, claim that he was not quite the full shilling. He was very kind to Cousin Rachael, especially when she contracted TB and had to go into a sanatorium. He had an old car. He lent it to Rachael once and she knocked over the petrol pump when she went to fill it with petrol!

* * *

Before I end this part, I should mention that after Robert and Elizabeth Tooth had seemingly been reduced to very difficult circumstances, other members of the family helped out, at least by giving assistance to their eight children, the ones I've just been speaking of. In 1885, after Robert Tooth was declared bankrupt, the sum of seven thousand pounds was settled on the children. It was provided in equal shares by three men - Robert's brother, Frederick, Robert Lucas Tooth, Robert's nephew, Edwin's son (who later became the first Baronet, but that's too complicated a story to tell here), and James Sutherland Mitchell, who was a partner in the Tooths' Sydney brewing firm. The money could be used for the children's education or settled on them directly when the youngest reached twenty-one. It must have been galling for Robert Tooth, once so powerful and wealthy, for this to happen. The children, however, did receive a good education, many of them at Bedford School.

CHAPTER 4

Now back to my father and mother, Henry Hazard and Margot. The wedding was at St. Matthew's, Westminster, which was a fashionable church then, and I suppose it does point to something in my father that speaks of wanting to rise above his station, although it probably suited the Tooths to have it at that venue. The Vicar from Harleston the Rev W H Cleaver came down to take the service. My father was thirty-five and my mother twenty. They went straight away to Pulham St Mary's, very close to Harleston, where my father took possession of a fine house known as 'Harrolds'.

I find it very difficult to write about Mother and Father, but as this is something of a family history, I suppose I have to be honest and say that though I loved them both, they did not love each other in the way I longed for them to. I'm sure my father was very fond of my mother, but my mother seemed to hold herself at a distance from my father. There was a shadow between them, which I can see more clearly now than when I was at home with them. Father was a very complicated person. He was always trying to impress. He lost his mother, of course, when he was very small and spent a lot of time with his grandparents, the Porters, in Ipswich. That must have been difficult for him. One little episode shows something of what life was like for him in Ipswich. They were having prunes and custard with dinner. Father couldn't stand prunes, but loved custard. He made himself eat all the prunes first, leaving the custard for sheer delight. He was about to enter into his joy when a voice came from the head of the table, "Take Master Henry's plate away." That's become a favourite tale in our family. Poor little boy! But Father himself became very autocratic. Perhaps it was to cover some personal insecurity in himself. One little incident from my childhood bears this out, I believe. Father at one time was furious because one man in the congregation at church (*his* church, the Hazards' church!) – the blacksmith – used to sing the hymns at the top of his voice and terribly out of tune. At table one Sunday lunch, Father was ranting about how this destroyed the beauty of the service and vowed to write a letter to the Vicar demanding that this man not be allowed to sing. We all begged him not to, but he would listen to no one, got up, dashed off the letter and stormed out to post it, our beseechings ringing in his ears. He returned some time later, looking very sour. Next Sunday the blacksmith was there in church singing as loudly and as badly as ever. We all looked at each other. I'm sure Father never posted the letter, but he had to maintain his standing within the family. Father was always on edge. Once he rowed with the Vicar and we all had to go to church in another village until the storm blew over. I remember another time when I was behaving badly at the table, scribbling in my notebook. My father ordered me to stop, but I carried on, being as wilful as I could be. Finally, I threw the notebook down and rushed out of the room in a tantrum. Father looked at what I had written – 'Father is mad, Father is mad', over and over again!

My mother was so different. I can't think what my father thought when Mother, who was Secretary of the local branch of the Suffragettes, brought Emmeline Pankhurst, to speak in

Harleston. Mother was sometimes on the point of leaving my father. She had a lot to put up with. When my sister Rosalind was born, Mother wanted to call her Diana. This was like a red rag to a bull for Father. Diana, a pagan name from Roman mythology! For weeks the argument went on, the baby remaining unregistered all the while. Rosalind is a good old English name, my father declared. He wouldn't give in. Eventually Mother backed down out of weariness. In that way my sister became Rosalind Anne. There was always an atmosphere of unpleasantness between Father and Mother, although I tried to insulate myself from it. I didn't realise it at the time, but I think it was because of this that we were sent away such a lot for our schooling.

Perhaps the difference in age was too great, or there was a distance between the Hazards and the Tooths that just couldn't be bridged. It's not as if my mother was clinging to her own family. She actually moved more and more away from them, in spirit at any rate. She was wont to refer to her own father as 'the beer baron'. Maybe it was my grandmother, Elizabeth Mansfield, coming through, because the shrewdness and hard-headedness one can see in the Tooths up to that time is not to be seen in my mother, Margot, nor any of her brothers or sisters. Maybe the Hazard element outweighed the Tooth element in that generation and from then onwards.

My mother, Margot, must have been almost swamped by the people around her. She had her own home and family, the seven of us. Her seven brothers and sisters kept appearing and re-appearing in her life, together with their families. Then, on top of all that, she had fourteen aunts and uncles mostly in England, but in Australia as well, with spouses and descendants almost too numerous to count. Beyond that, again, were all the Hazard relations. She kept in touch with this huge family. Some were called into service as godparents for her children. Each one of us had the statutory three godparents – twenty-one in all. Not one was called to stand twice. My own godparents were my mother's cousin by marriage, Sydney Nevile (who later became Sir Sydney), her cousin, Ada Porter, from my father's side of the family, and Katherine Candler, another cousin from the Hazard side. One of my fondest possessions still is a tiny, silver-covered prayer book that belonged to Katherine Candler.

Margot Hazard wearing one of her own shawls

My four older brothers and sister and I were born at Harrold's, Pulham St Mary's, and it wasn't until we moved into Caltofts that the last two were born. That made up the seven of us. Then began a time at Caltofts which, despite the difficulties I've been speaking of, I look back on as the golden age of my life. O that it might have gone on for ever!

To begin with, there was the house itself. It's an old house, parts of it hundreds of years old. In my mind, I go back to it again and again. I walk through the little side door, into the hall. I wander through the dining room and run my hand over the beautiful panelling and the enormous sideboard. Then into the drawing room and the sitting room with the French windows opening on to the garden. I climb the stairs once more, remembering our shrieks as we sailed down the banisters in the years gone by. I walk to the 'new wing', into my room. There's the length of string I used to tie to my big toe and leave dangling down outside so the gardener could wake me early in the morning by tugging on it. Then to Janet's, next door, and to Noel's, where I stop to say a prayer for him. I hear Cousin Audrey's giggle as we creep downstairs, off at 5.00 am to bathe - stark naked! - in the Waveney. Now I'm in the nursery. Nurse Skinner, so nice yet so strict – we loved her! – keeping us in order. (Sometimes we were given a treat. After our porridge or bread and milk we would be allowed downstairs while Father was still at table. He'd cut the top off his egg and give it to one of us! Then we would be sent into the garden to play – but not on the wet grass! We had to keep together, and always include Christopher!). Downstairs again, I wander into the conservatory, through the gardens, past the pond, to the tennis court. I stand by the rockery we children helped to build. Yellow dog Bingo comes bounding up to me. Then along to the stables. The pony, Antony, whinnies to me. Robert, who cared for us so loyally and for so long, is standing there, reins in hand, beside the spring cart that my mother loved to ride in. Robert goes to feed the goats – Miss Briggs, Martha and Mary. Robert's wife – 'Mrs Robert' – used to look after us on Nurse's day off. What fun we had with her! There was a harrowing old poem she would recite to us, keeping us in fits of laughter. It was about a poor couple who had to choose one of their seven children to give away in exchange for a free house and land for the rest of their life. Seven, like us! It begins,

> "Which shall it be? Which shall it be?
> I looked at John, John looked at me."

Those words will be with me all the days of my life! In the end, they can't bring themselves to part with any of them, of course.

What fun we had! In the holidays, especially, when everyone was home! Dressing up, plays, charades, concerts, rounders, expeditions to the river. Do other children now play, as we did, happy as kings, there on the river? In the summer, Father sometimes took a house at Southwold for all of us. The days were endless! How excited we were when our cousins, Audrey and Kit Candler, came to Caltofts! To church on Sunday, in the Hazard pew. Val, with his Caltofts Courier – 'the Paper with the smallest circulation in the World' and his reports of 'Mrs Hazard's Garden Party' or 'Mr W.H. Hazard's Success at the Weybread Rifle Club'. There's Father, off to a parade of the

Volunteer Brigade. I have with me now the silver card-tray his men gave him for his marriage. Or I picture him coming in from tennis or returning from a Lodge meeting, or with camera and tripod in hand, setting out on a ramble. And there's my mother, sitting placidly in the sunshine, spinning, or at her loom, weaving her beautiful fabrics, her stillness contrasting with my father's constant activity. She goes to speak to our governess, Miss Saunders, or to Emily or Margaret, the maids. I remember the thrill I'd feel when Mother would come to the Nursery to say good-night, her coffee-smell so strong. I can *feel* it now! In a different vision, there is Mother in the parlour at a Suffragette meeting. How we laughed at the advertisement in the Caltofts Courier – 'Wanted. Any reliable strong man or woman to join our Anti-Suffragette League'!

* * *

Noel was the first-born of us. William Noel. He was very handsome and grew to be well over six feet. He was my hero. All of us adored him. His first school was Eversley, in Southwold, and he used to bring home prizes from there. He went on to Lancing and did very well. He won the Modern Languages Prize in his final year, I know, and won a scholarship to Oxford to do Mathematics, but didn't take it up. He was destined to succeed his father in the law practice, and began work there after a stint with a big London firm, but then the war intervened. Noel was twenty-one. After enlisting in January, 1916, he served in the Dragoon Guards, then, in September, 1917, won a commission as a second lieutenant in the 14th Battalion, Welsh Regiment, and won a Meritorious Service Medal for distinguished bravery in France. He was killed in action ten weeks before the war ended. The night he died, and, of course, before the news reached us – we were on holiday at Sheringham - he came to me and called my name three times, "Joyce! Joyce! Joyce!" Noel is buried in the Lone Ridge British Cemetery at Longueval, and his name is on the village memorial outside the church, alongside Caltofts. I think of him every day.

Val was also at Lancing. Robert Valentine, to give him his full name. Whereas Noel was strong and very masculine, if I could put it like that – and very clever, Val had a more imaginative mind. When we were children, he was the one who would put on our concerts. We acted his plays and sang the songs he wrote. I still have many of his poems and plays. At Lancing, he won the Poetry Prize in his final year, with 'The Masque of War', a long reflective work filled with classical Greek allusions. Later on, even while he was at the war, he wrote marvellous stories and poems, some of which were published in different journals. He wrote occasionally under the pseudonym, John Plowman. He was an intellectual, you could say, but also an athlete, and won prizes for cross-country running when he was in the Middle East. Val was also very handsome, and caught the eye of the young ladies. He had quite an eye for them in return. He used to flirt outrageously, with married women as well as unmarried, other people have told me. Val served in a Machine Gun Corps on the Western Front for some time, but mostly in the Middle East, and played a small but very brave – and important - part in the First Battle of Gaza. Under fire he rescued the baggage animals from danger, without loss of life to man or beast. After the war, Val transferred to the 2nd Battalion, Norfolk Regiment, as a Second-Lieutenant. He served first in Russia in that curious war between the Whites and the Reds. He came back to Harleston after that, but was appalled at how things were in the family. I think he might have been disappointed in love as well, so he re-signed with the Regiment. That took him to various places in India and the Middle East, including the ancient biblical city of Ur of the Chaldees. When he was there he picked up ('stole' is the right word, actually!) a lovely small figurine carved in alabaster, exactly the same as you see in the British Museum, dating back thousands of years. It's been passed on in the family, though I'd better not say where it is now! The Regiment was then posted to West Africa. In 1925, I received the awful news that Val had died at Calabar in Nigeria after becoming ill with yellow fever. My father composed the wording for his memorial in the church in Calabar: 'He feared God and honoured his King. He served his country faithfully in War and Peace in England, Egypt, France, Russia, India, Mesopotamia, and Nigeria. The souls of the righteous are in the hands of God'. Val left his estate to his father – £349. So my two brave brothers were cut short in their untarnished youth. And another link with my homeland was broken.

After Val came Janet, with whom it seems my life is to be linked more than with any of the others, as she has followed me here to Australia. Janet was christened Janet Mary Marguerite. Like me, she has marvellous recollections of our childhood at Caltofts. Janet once said she dreamt of Caltofts every night of her life. She and I were at a small school in Lowestoft together. Charlie was at another school nearby at the same time. Janet

Lieutenant Robert Valentine Hazard

Lancing College cadets in camp, Farnborough, Hampshire, 4 August, 1913. Val is front right. The Great War started exactly one year later

went to St Felix in Southwold for the last two years of her schooling, and I joined her there also. After school, she studied horticulture at Swanley, where she made good friends like Alfreda Johns from Wales. Janet was tall, like most of us Hazards. I envied her calmness and patience, her steadiness, because these are the qualities I seem not to have. I'm driven by my feelings and form quick and strong impressions, whereas Janet is balanced and thoughtful, and seems to understand herself. After the war, my father and my sister Janet made a pilgrimage to Noel's grave in Western France. It was a nightmare trip in the awful conditions that still existed, but Janet had a wonderful experience during the journey. She fell one day into a waking dream in which she had what I'd have to call a vision. The Virgin Mary appeared to her and gave her a message that she would have a life of great difficulty, but that in the end, when life was over, all would be well for her. The vision gradually faded, but Janet was left with an absolute assurance that the prophecy would be fulfilled.

Charlie was the next above me. Charles Gower Hazard. Charlie was the odd one out, and he lived a very difficult life. He used to act strangely and would get into rages. He threatened to burn the house down on one occasion. He was at his best when rambling in the countryside, and often took his ferrets with him. He shocked the household when he tried to kiss Audrey McGeagh on the stairs, which doesn't seem so terrible from this distance, but Audrey was banned from Caltofts as a result! When he was ten he was sent away to a small boarding school in Lowestoft, and later to Haileybury for a time, but he never did well. He was too dreamy for academic work. The war was

Janet on her motorbike, 'Chitty', 1924

Joyce and Janet in front of St Felix, Southwold. Janet, Joyce and Rosalind were all day-girls here at various times in their schooldays

Janet driving Margot and Rosalind, 1922. Whose car?

on while he was at Haileybury, and although he was only seventeen, he wanted desperately to join Noel and Val in the forces. Some heartless person on the train gave him a white feather. Charlie was deeply upset by this. My father arranged for him to be articled to the same London firm of lawyers that Noel had started with, but it was impossible. He was thrown out of the firm and out of his lodgings. Father took him on as an articled clerk, but things went from bad to worse. He fought with his father. His condition was deteriorating and eventually it became so bad that he was put into a special place for mentally-disturbed people at Thorpe, near Norwich, suffering from schizophrenia. There was one terrible time when he imprisoned himself there, and demanded that five shillings be sent to him. Then he took his glasses and ground them up into little pieces. Both Janet and I have felt badly that we couldn't do anything for Charlie so far away, but we have to make decisions in our lives, and we have made ours.

Then me, Joyce Winifred. I was born in April in 1901, just before we moved into Caltofts. There are many photographs of us children, and I'm the one who always looks self-conscious and unsure of myself. I think I have quite a lot of Val's imagination and writing ability, though I find it hard to write about myself. I was at St Felix from before the war until after it ended. Janet was there with me for the first two years and Rosalind for most of my last years. I went through to the Sixth Form and went up to London afterwards. I'd go and stay with different ones of my relations for quite long periods. It was in that queer time just after the war. Underneath, I was still feeling Noel's death, but I was putting on a bold front. Others would have thought of me as just erratic, probably. I had a motor-bike for a while – I called it 'Prue' - and did some dopey things. Dopey for me, at any rate. I went by the name, 'Sybil' for a time. Perhaps I was trying to get away from my past. Then, when everything collapsed at home, and with despair on all fronts, I made a mad decision to sail away from it all. That's how I come to be in Australia!

Joyce Winifred Hazard on the eve of her leaving England, 1923. Are these the glasses she smashed at Waltons, near Ballarat, the following year?

Thank goodness Christopher was too young to go to war. He was christened Christopher Martin Hazard. Christopher was sent off to Oundle, but he had a hard time there. Like Val and me, he has a lively and inventive mind, but he stammers quite badly. After Magdalene College, Cambridge, he trained as a teacher. I'm very fond of Christopher, but we didn't see much of each other before I left to come to Australia.

Finally, there's Rosalind, the youngest of the seven of us, or Rosalind Anne, the one who was nearly 'Diana'. Rosalind had a very mixed schooling. When she was seven, she was sent off to the Morley-Smiths nearby to share a governess with Dorothy. Dorothy Morley-Smith was the only surviving child of seven, and she, poor thing, died when she was fourteen. Then there was a similar arrangement with the Fenns, except that there were several little children there. Rosalind came to St Felix School in Southwold as a day-girl with Janet and me. She was still very young, and in 1915, when she was nine, she and Janet both left and went to Norwich High School for a time. Rosalind then spent a year with the O'Briens – Emma and Mary - near Farnham in Surrey and went to a dame school. (Mary O'Brien and Edith Morley-Smith were Janet's godmothers). Rosalind then came back to Saint Felix just before I left and remained there as a boarder until the end of 1921, when she was nearly sixteen. Her time at the school was cut short by our father's financial collapse. Rosalind was very good to our mother and father after the dam broke. After all, who else was there, with Noel and Val gone, Janet and I out here, and Charlie unable to do anything? There were only Christopher and Rosalind, and

Christopher was making his way in life. At any rate, he was going through a very unsettled time in his life, as I had done.

* * *

In 1923, I made that 'mad decision' to leave home and homeland. I came out with Jill Kendall whom I had known, together with her sister, Vivien, after Vivien came to live at Caltofts while learning weaving from my mother. Jill was impetuous and headstrong, and I was carried along in her train, although I don't want to escape the responsibility for my decision. I was older than she was, after all. We travelled on the Largs Bay, and arrived in Melbourne in the middle of winter. Vivien came later, in 1925, with her mother, Mrs Kendall– and stayed here. She is my close friend. There are so many stories to tell about Vivien, but they will have to be left for another time. What a life she led! My sister Janet, as I've said, came out here the year after me. She doesn't say it openly, but I have an idea she was sent out here by my mother to make sure I was all right, after my madcap departure. It seems, though, that that has resulted in my mother losing two daughters rather than one!

There I will leave you, or you me. I don't want to carry my own story any further. That will be up to others. Not only am I in Australia, but beginning to think of myself as Australian. I suppose I should feel so, because in 1924, I cast my lot with my new country irrevocably through my marriage to a man who is as Australian as I felt myself to be English up to the day of my marriage.

A view of Caltofts from the garden, about 1900

Robert, the groom, with Margot Hazard, Noel (on horseback), Val, and Nurse, probably 1897

Caltofts from the garden. Date unknown

Caltofts from the tennis court

Robert, the groom, with various children, including some Hazards

Janet with Miss Briggs, Martha and Mary

William Henry and Margot Hazard with (l-r) Val, Noel, Janet, Charlie, and Joyce. Off to church for the baptism, 22 May, 1901

William Henry Hazard at the front door, Caltofts

Dressing up at Caltofts. Left to Right: Charlie (?), Miss Saunders (governess), Christopher, Janet, Joyce, Rosalind

William Henry Hazard was a camera enthusiast

In the conservatory, Caltofts, 1904. From (l-r): Joyce, Charlie, Christopher, Janet. Val and Noel are at the back. Rosalind is yet to be born

The Hazard family just prior to the First World War, with ages. Back (l-r) Joyce (12), Charlie (13), Janet (15). Middle (l-r) Val 18, Margot (43), Henry (56), Noel (20). Front (l-r) Christopher (10), Rosalind (7)

PART 3. WATTLE

CHAPTER 1

JAMES TIMOTHY CONNELLY

I'm beginning this continuation of the family story on the ninetieth anniversary of my parents' wedding. That's where they each ended their contribution, as you will have read. That was 1924, and it's now 2014. Although I'll be reaching back over those ninety years, it's from the perspective of the present time that I'm writing.

There's a lot to write about. My mother and father had thirty-seven years together, to begin with, and that takes us only to 1961, when my father died. To avoid having what they wrote about cut off abruptly or left hanging in the air, I will need to follow through with some of the people and the events they mentioned. Then to carry the story further.

I'm Jim Connelly, the fourth and final product of that marriage, and I'll try to write on behalf of my remaining sister and brother, but everything I write is from my own viewpoint.

* * *

When my dad returned from the First World War, he was suffering from some sort of post-war trauma, I feel sure. He told how he did nothing but sit around and eat up his war gratuity in the months following his return. But it was more than that. He could have obtained some land under the Soldier Settlement arrangements. Several large properties around Ballarat were being cut up for soldier settlement, including the big 'Ercildoune' property, which was close to Learmonth and which he knew very well. Many local men received blocks of land there. But Dad refused even to apply. 'I want no farm,' he told his cousin, Mary McMahon. I can see something stubbornly Irish as well as something personally unhealthy in that. His war experiences were traumatic enough as an explanation, I believe – the conditions on the Western front, the awfulness of front-line trench warfare, and his long period as a prisoner-of-war. Dad never spoke much about his war experience. He did describe to me once just how he and the others were taken prisoner, and he kept one or two war souvenirs like a German belt buckle, but he would never be a part of the RSL, nor march on Anzac Day, nor anything like that. He did, however, eventually settle down to work in those post-war years. In about 1923 or 1924, he was working as a farm-hand on a property near Windermere, not far from Learmonth. That is where his life intersected with my mother's.

Dad (l) and Mr Swan, on Mr Swan's property, 1924?

My mother, together with Jill Kendall, left London on the *Largs Bay* on the twenty-sixth of June, 1923. The 'Largs Bay,' almost brand new, was built for the Australian Government specifically to bring migrants from Britain. On that trip, the ship was carrying over seven hundred migrants, almost all young unmarried men and women. The largest categories according to the ship's manifest were farm workers, farm learners, 'lads', and domestics. There was another category – 'lady helps', only four in number, and including Joyce W. Hazard and Rosemary Kendall. (Rosemary was Jill's real name). It would seem that these four were chosen for some kind of 'superior' domestic service on account of their 'superior' backgrounds. After their arrival in Melbourne on the second of August, 1923, my mother and Jill soon parted. Mum went to a job caring for the three small Hutton children on their farm at Swifts Creek, nearly 400 kilometres east of Melbourne. Perhaps this was a position assigned to her as part of the migration protocols. Swifts Creek is a cold and bleak place, but the photos show a happy group of children with their pony. Something seems to have gone wrong, however, because my mother didn't stay long. It's been suggested that a broken love attachment may have been the cause, and if that is so, it helps to explain what happened shortly after.

My mother moved on to a position with the Swan family, who had a property, 'Rosedale', at Cardigan, not far from Ballarat and about four kilometres from where Dad was working on a property called 'Windermere'. He, too, had a lost love. He had fallen in love with the daughter of the place where he was working at the time. The girl used to visit the Connellys at their place at Weatherboard. However, her family was Protestant, and the father objected to the romance because Dad was Catholic. He sacked Dad, and ordered his daughter to break off the relationship. The girl married another farmer next door. The irony is that her father died a month later. I suppose you could say that my father and mother, Will and Joyce, caught each other on the rebound. The memory of 'the other girl' seemed to linger in Dad's mind. Someone said his personality changed as a result of what had happened. My mother felt she was living in the shadow of Dad's former love. She said to someone later on, "Will never loved me. I'm sure he loved that other girl better." Mrs Swan wrote a letter to my mother's mother in England in which she expressed her disapproval of the marriage, but it was too late. The wedding was over before the letter was received.

I have a letter written by my mother to my father in July, 1924, only a short time before their wedding. It says so much about them both (my father by his silence!)

Dearest Con,

It is letter-day again already. No letter from you, though. I expect it will come tomorrow. I went to fetch it on Jenny, too, & Jenny must have known there wouldn't be one, for she absolutely crawled, & nothing could spur her on. The telephone has come, and is put into the dining-room, will you ring me up some time? Cardigan 5 is the number, only I'm afraid you are nowhere near a telephone, so then you couldn't, of course.

I drove Mrs. Swan to Waltons yesterday, Ethel was picking up potatoes for the diggers, & did not come in at all, so I only saw her from a distance. They gave her fourpence a bag, & she got six shillings on Tuesday afternoon! Mr. Swan said he would give me a shilling a bag for digging ours, so I said all right, & went and started this afternoon, in joy and gladness. But all the ones I could find were the size of peas, so I didn't get my bag full! Anyhow it rained, so I came in again before an hour was up. Here is a rhyme I made up while I was doing it:

> *There once was a terrible dud,*
> *Who decided to dig for a spud.*
> *He dug a whole day,*
> *But without any pay,*
> *For he couldn't find nothing but mud.*

This pen won't write tonight, or else it is the fault of the paper. I have told Mrs. Swan about next Sunday week, so that is all right. She was ill on Monday, so I forgave her for her horridness on Sunday, & since then we have been friends again. It won't last, of course. I made another cake on Tuesday, not a good one, though, the oven was too cool. I'm going to do the same cake again tomorrow, & get it right this time.

Won't it be <u>fun</u> when you come & fetch me in the gig on Sunday week? It will really be the first time we have been *out together. I suppose that makes it more exciting still. I am excited, anyway, do be excited too.*

I smashed my glasses at Waltons, settled them this time, & they had to go to Ballarat to be mended. It is maddening, just when I was trying so hard to make both ends meet, to have one end getting still further away like that. I suppose the blooming things will cost nearly a pound, blow them, & as soon as I get them back I shall smash them again probably. Glasses are more trouble than they are worth.

I am just so sleepy that I can't string my words together, I'm afraid. I'll have to stop.

The rest of the letter is missing. I wonder if it was ever finished and if it was ever sent.

*   *   *

The wedding was at St. Patrick's Catholic Cathedral in Ballarat. The date was the twentieth of August, 1924, only six and a half weeks after the letter shown above was written. My father's cousin, Maggie Ryan, and his faithful old uncle, Pat Connelly, stood witness for them. My mother had been staying with Maggie and Pat Ryan just before the wedding. Mum was received into the Catholic Church at some time before the ceremony. Given her own and her family's deep association with the Church of England, that was a remarkable thing. Was it at least in part due to her desire to make a clean break with the trappings of her past? After the wedding the two of them had tea with Annie and Pat at the old house – sausages and mashed potatoes – then returned right across the road to the place they had rented from the Hendersons. There was a tin-kettling for the newly-married couple, as was the custom then. People brought sandwiches and cakes, and my father got in a barrel of beer. "All the old drunks around Weatherboard were there," according to someone who was present. Dad was thirty-two and Mum was twenty-three at the time.

The first years were difficult for my mother. She was the newcomer amongst a family with fixed routines and a common culture – an Englishwoman amongst Irish folk, a recent Protestant amongst Catholics. A good example of her acute sense of being made to feel an outsider is to be found in the card games. The Connellys were experienced and cunning card players. Mum didn't know their games – euchre and five hundred. She was understandably nervous and clumsy, but no allowances were made for her. The women in the family used to gather every week at the old homestead for a baking day. They'd bring their own supplies, share things and talk, and take their own goods home. It would appear to be another difficult scene for my mother to fit into. It must have been with a sense of relief that she and Dad moved away soon afterwards.

My mother continued as a steadfast member of the Catholic Church for some years, although Dad seldom attended. He would drive Mum to church in the gig, go round to a friend's house until church was over, then pick her up and drive her home. The issue of Mum's church membership became acute when the children started to arrive. Mum had several miscarriages before Tessy was born in April, 1927. Angela arrived fourteen months later, in June, 1928. Then came Noel in October, 1930. By this time my mother was fed up with the fact that, though she had 'changed' for Dad, he was not involved in any way with the church. She came to regret her original decision. As well, it is reasonable to assume that with the perspective of distance and increasing maturity, she was feeling the call of the church she had grown up in. She finally announced to Dad that she was going to return to her own church. There was something of a scene, which ended with Dad saying, "You can do what you like with the others, but you're not going to take Noel." That was the status quo when I arrived in July, 1933. The first three children were baptised in the Catholic Church, but I was baptised in the Church of England, at Dingley, near Pearcedale, where the family was then living. The Catholic genesis of the three older children soon evaporated, including Noel's, and they went on to live their lives as thoroughly Protestant. Even Dad, when he was in hospital nearing the end of his life, when asked to put down his religion, wrote 'Church of England'.

CHAPTER 2

After a short time at Cardigan, Dad and Mum moved to a place at Creswick North, twenty kilometres or so away. That was towards the end of 1925. They remained there for seven years. Somehow or other they scraped up the money to buy it, either when they first went or during the time they were living there. Dad got a job with the School of Forestry, though it was not full-time work. The Forestry School had been established in 1910, and at that time its chief work was to produce seedlings for establishing plantations throughout the State. Dad was proud of his connection with the School and maintained an interest in forestry all his life. Mum, of course, was at home, with the three children. They lived several kilometres from the town of Creswick itself, and in a quite isolated place, although there was a lively social life in the manner of country living at that time. The Common was opposite the house, covered with gorse, but it was a playing space for the children rather than a barrier. The Kennedys lived nearby. Mavis Poland was a friend of the children, and the two families got on well. They bought butter from Mrs Merriman, who lived with her handicapped son. Mrs Merriman once lost her false teeth, but the story ended happily when they were discovered in a customer's pound of butter. Tessy and Angela, to their own and their mother's shame, once called out rude things to an old woman who lived along the road. Mum made them go and apologise. Some time later, the woman's house burnt down, and the children felt mortified that they had treated the poor woman so badly.

Dad and Mum (holding 'Chuff'), with Vivien (front) and Jill Kendall, 1926?

Tessy and Angela, North Creswick, 1929

It was a happy family time, perhaps the best years of all, despite the hardship of the Depression years. Mum and Dad each had their own garden – narrow beds with paths between. Tessy and Angela had fun jumping over the beds on to the solid ground on the other side. Dad grew radishes and had a border of flowers. Mum grew cress, sown in the shape of a T for Tessy, A for Angela, and N for Noel. The children had a swing suspended from a large tree in the garden. There was a black dog called Chuff. Mum and Dad disputed which of them the dog was more attached to. One day, when they were walking, they came to a fork in the road and decided to test the dog's affections; one walked one way, the other walked the other way. There's no known end to the story, unfortunately. Perhaps the dog sat on its tail in confusion. Noel distinguished himself by going to the baker's for a loaf of bread, then eating all the inside on the way home, leaving only the hollow crust. On another occasion, he caught his jumper on the barbed wire as he was crawling under a fence, and lay there, contentedly, for hours, until someone came to rescue him. One terrible time, Angela, playing hide-and-seek, got herself into a drum standing in a corner of the kitchen, and couldn't get out. She was in great pain. The more Mum and Dad tried to manoeuvre her out, the more firmly she was trapped. They got Mr Tassiker to come with his car and drive her to the garage, where she was eventually freed by delicately cutting the drum open. Angela's legs were quite numb, and she collapsed on the floor. Afterwards, Mum wrote one of her poems about it. She wrote it in quite jocular fashion, ending by lamenting the loss of her oil drum. Angela feels quite aggrieved. Tessy and Angela both went to school at North Creswick, a longish walk for them. They were bright children.

Tessy, at the age of three, is reputed to have read an advertisement in the paper, and commented, "Men's fleecy underpants, 2/6. That's cheap!" At six, she wrote her own absence note to the teacher after being away from school.

As well as his work at the School of Forestry, Dad was doing farm work as well. I think he must have been called in by the Forestry when extra labour was needed. As the effects of the Great Depression began to deepen after 1929, money was very tight in the community and in the Connelly household. Dad kept a little black notebook in which he jotted down a great variety of things, from cricket scores to prices of stock feed and the correct dimensions of poultry sheds. In 1930, he listed his wages as follows

Harvest	£7/0/0
Cropping	£30/0/0
Spud digging	£37/0/0
Plantations	£17/6/0
Shearing	£3/7/6
Ploughing	£0/10/0
Fencing	£1/7/6
Wood carting	£2/14/0
Stick carting	£2/8/6
Total	£101/8/6

Family income varied from year to year. Dad's wages the previous year were £154. In the year following, £123. One can imagine my mother's anxieties in providing for the young family amidst such uncertainty. The house cow, Amy, was a blessing. She calved, according to the notebook, on Sunday, 3rd August. There were also the chooks. Dad recorded that he set the first hen on twelve Black Orpington eggs on 24th July; there were nine chicks. The second hen sat on twelve eggs on 29 September; six chicks hatched; and so on with the other hens.

Noel was born in October, 1930, in the depths of the Depression. There were poignant moments. Angela was given some pieces of money to buy sugar at the shop. She came back with a minute quantity, and said, "Mummy, I lost all those little bits you gave me except one, and here's the sugar." There were, however, lighter moments as well. There are photos from this time of the family in the gardens in Ballarat, the two girls sitting astride the lion statues. Vivien, always 'Aunty Vivien' to us, would come from Melbourne to visit. And our Aunty Janet, Mum's s sister, married and came to live in Creswick, although we moved away shortly afterwards. In fact, the place was sold to Janet and her husband, Tom Mason. The selling price was £20, according to Mason family folk lore.

CHAPTER 3

In 1932, after seven years at Creswick North, there was a major upheaval. The family moved to Pearcedale, nearly two hundred kilometres away. Pearcedale is on the Mornington Peninsula, further from Creswick than that distance suggests, because the metropolis of Melbourne lies between them, a significant barrier. Was my mother pleased to get away from the Ballarat district, with its long Connelly associations? The reason for removal, however, may have been more positive. The Mornington Peninsula was a rapidly developing region, thought of as the place of the future. It was a bold decision to make that move, and speaks well of my parents. My father acted decisively. He drove a horse and jinker down there to spy out the possibilities. Right through the middle of Melbourne he drove, down Swanston Street and over Princes Bridge. Did he camp out at night, I wonder? He found a house and some land there at Pearcedale, and bought it.

There is a mystery as to how the money was raised to buy the property. Twenty pounds would hardly have done it. We can rule out any accumulated money from within the family itself. We can also rule out anything coming from my mother's family in England. Her parents' letters at this time seem to indicate that there was nothing to spare. The sale of Caltofts had done nothing more than pay off her father's liabilities. Some in the family say that our mother had some jewels which she sold to raise the money. This seems very doubtful, given her own and her family's impoverishment. Perhaps Dad's Uncle Pat helped out. My father seems to have been in good standing with him. Or was there some money from Mum's Aunt Winnie or Aunt Anna?

I was born the following year, in July, 1933, completing the family. Tessy was six, Angela five, and Noel almost three. My birth is better documented than the others', as our Aunty Vivien has written about it. My mother felt certain that the birth was going to mean curtains for her. As a result, she decided to have the birth in the Women's Hospital in Melbourne. Tessy, Angela, and Noel were packed off to the Andreasons in Dingley, and my mother went to stay with Aunty Vivien in Williamstown to await the birth. In her letter, Aunty Vivien goes on:

> *To say money was short was putting it mildly. It was practically non-existent. We couldn't afford to light the fire (this was July) until the evening and then it was mostly with driftwood we'd picked up on the beach. ... About 11 AM the sun would shine into one corner of the garden. We'd wait for this and rush out with a chair each to sit and bask, your mother teaching me to crochet and me teaching her to knit. At last one Saturday evening she thought the time had come, so we walked over to the station. I couldn't accompany her as Gerry was in bed asleep. I've never forgotten her agonised face as she sat in the carriage and drew away from me.*

However, there were no complications, and a ten-pound baby resulted! I was born with a caul over my face, which means I am immune from drowning.

* * *

The Pearcedale block had the house and some thirty acres, and Dad hoped to make a living from it. There was an orchard of sorts and there were the chooks. 400 day-old chickens were ordered from Lakelins and cost £13/15/0. In his notebook, Dad noted down the correct feed ratios for adult birds: pollard six parts, bran three parts, meatmeal one part. There were one or two cows as well. But the pigs were the main thing. Pens were built, and a slaughterhouse as well. Dad went about his work very methodically. "If you buy pigs with dry skin, give one part each of bone and sulphur for a day, and then feed on meat and meat soup," he copied into his notebook. The land was not good. The Parkers, who lived at the back of our place and became friends, had better land. Tessy and Angela were at school, and Noel started school there. Gordon Parker used to look after him. The Andreasons were other friends, despite living some distance away. Mr Andreason was Norwegian, and built a beautiful model ship in a glass case, which Noel has now. The daughter, Mavis Andreason, was sole godmother at my baptism in Christ Church, Dingley (Church of England!) a few months after I was born, but a great shadow fell on her. My mother had a quite significant stamp collection that had come down in her family. One day a valuable stamp from it was found to be missing. Suspicion fell on Mavis Andreason.

But the Pearcedale venture failed. It couldn't bring in enough money, and soon Dad was off working elsewhere, mainly digging potatoes on the Koo Wee Rup Swamp and around Neerim South. The failure at Pearcedale must have been a bad blow to Dad. This had been his chance. Despite his former protestations, his Irish background, strong in all of us Connellys, must have stirred within him as he at last farmed his own land. Then he lost it, and had to go back on to rented properties. When the opportunity arose, years later, to once again buy some land, it was through the generosity of my mother's friends that it came. I think the defeated aura that accompanied him in later years might have originated here. Early in 1935, the family sold up, salvaged what they could, and moved to a little place a kilometre or two south of the little township of Garfield in West Gippsland, fifty kilometres away. They had been less than two years at Pearcedale.

CHAPTER 4

It is time to return to the fortunes of my mother's father and mother in England. My mother left England in 1923, five years after the end of the Great War. The war was the cause of her father's financial collapse, though it may have been that he was over-stretched before the war began. He seemed to have something in his character that drove him to reach beyond himself. He had, for instance, earlier purchased the Lordship of the Manor of Harleston, which had once belonged to his uncle, Christopher Martin Hazard, and which had no meaning other than status. Occasionally he would attach the title, 'Lord' to his signature on official documents. One understanding in the family is that before the war and perhaps in the early stages of the war he advised clients to invest in Russian securities. Perhaps he did the same himself. When the Russian state dissolved into anarchy and then communism, these moneys were irretrievably lost. Further, however, he insisted on compensating the clients who had acted on his advice from his own resources, thus beggaring himself. Others believe he lost his money by investing in Brazilian railways. There was some contraction in British railway investment in Brazil at that time. One railway company did go bankrupt in 1914, although there was no major downturn. There is another rumour of doubtful practice, and that Henry's sister-in-law, Winnie, bailed him out of deeper trouble. Certainly she helped by paying him full value for shares that had lost their entire value. Perhaps he was simply an unwise investor. By the end of the war, Henry Hazard was sixty-one years old and no doubt exhausted and dispirited by all that had occurred. He and Margot moved out of Caltofts temporarily when it was pressed into service as a nursing home for convalescent soldiers during the last stage of the war. They returned and hung on there until early in 1925. Henry's law practice of Hazard and Pratt passed to the senior partner, Oswald Norman Martin, who moved into Caltofts, and carried on the practice for many years.

Mum's parents, Henry and Margot, together with Rosalind, were forced into rented accommodation wherever they could find it, moving from place to place over the years. At first they were at Peacehaven, an "awful place" between Brighton and Newhaven, built haphazardly towards the end of the war and named by the winner of a newspaper competition. (Its original name was 'New-Anzac-on-Sea'!) Rosalind used to ride her bicycle around looking for places for them to rent. This was before she went to Teachers College, which, as a sign of how things were, was paid for by family friends, the O'Briens, from Surrey. Early in 1926, Henry is writing to my mother from 'Green Shutters', Winchelsea, in Sussex. "I don't know where we shall find ourselves in April," he says. "We can't hear of a house about here and think of going west to Devonshire if we can find a house there." The air of gloom continues: "It is a horrid wet night, and we are very isolated on these marshes. I wish you were nearer." One can imagine the heartache such letters would have engendered in my mother. Henry died in May of the following year, 1927, leaving his estate to Margot. It was valued at the astonishing figure of 5996 pounds. Presumably, as Henry and Margot were living in rented houses and had no other income, they needed to preserve a capital sum to see them into the future. As well, Caltofts, which had yet to be sold, may have counted as an asset. Presumably, Henry had debts that would balance the capital value of Caltofts.

For some reason the sale of Caltofts did not occur until 1933. My mother's mother writes to her in April, 1933, from Reigate in Surrey (when Mum was five months pregnant with me):

> *My dearest Deusch,*
>
> *Do forgive me if you can for not writing more. Your sad life is always present to me, and if my life would help you, how willingly I would give it, but one cannot make those bargains. It seems so wearing for you if I say I am sorry too often. The sale of Caltofts was a dreadful disappointment. Nothing over! I had hoped for 100 pounds or more, which would have made all the difference. Janet sent me dear Tessie's little letter. What an intelligent child she is. She will be a very great comfort to you, darling. I was showing that last photograph of 'the three' to some friends the other day and they admired the children so much ...*

We can guess the kind of letters my mother was writing home during those years, and although we cannot see them, we can imagine how they compared with the tone of the letter Mum wrote to Dad just before they were married. The sense of gloom coming from Mum's parents continued and suggest that the situation here was deteriorating. Two months after the letter just quoted, Margot was writing again, this time from Aspley

Guise, Woburn Sands, in Bedfordshire. My mother was then staying with friends, probably the Andreasons, in Pearcedale.

My dearest Deusch,

You know how grieved for you everyone who loves you must feel. I am thankful that you are now with friends who will do all they can to help you till you have to go to Melbourne. Every time it is more trying in the last months and more urgent to rest if you can. You ought never to have this to bear again. I expect Tessie and Angel and little Noel are highly delighted to have this holiday. ... Is Will at home now? Did you have any difficulty in getting away? ... My dear child. God bless you. Your loving Mother.

* * *

Margot was a woman of considerable literary ability. Even during this time of distress, she was writing short stories, poems, and plays, drawing on her mother in choosing 'Jane Mansfield' as a pen-name. Some of them have come down to us. Several were sent for publication, unsuccessfully, it would seem. Writing her work in longhand, she would then have it typed it out before sending it off. The addresses shown on the various pieces show her to have been at Chelsea Cottage, Winchelsea, in early 1927, and at Ashley House, Five Oaks, Jersey, in 1929. One of her poems is indicative of Margot's literary sense. It is entitled, 'Song', and was suggested by some lines from Walt Whitman. 'Lila' is an Indian word meaning 'the Sport of God.'

Sing a song of spring-tide, flashing gold and blue
Amethyst and opal, emerald shimmering through -
White of burning brilliance, glowing crimson's hue.

    Lila Lila

Sound of footsteps dancing, tumultuous and free,
Sound of harps and viols, subdued in ecstasy,
Trumpets and shawms that shout aloud exultant minstrelsy.

    Lila Lila

Wilt thou not dance, Beloved? Our hands seek thine.
Upon this flower-decked sward we beckon thee
To dance with us till nightfall change the tune.
The music sounds in splendour of the spring,
The music echoes passing strange and sweet,
Dance thou with us till nightfall change the tune.

    Lila Lila

Sound of throbbing footsteps dancing, joyous, free,
Sound of all the bells that ring in April's ecstasy,
Sound of all the birds that flute in April's minstrelsy.

    Lila Lila

Sing a song of spring-tide, crystalline and blue,
Iris-hearted glory, shot with amber through,
Dazzling gold and purple, glowing crimson's hue.

    Lila Lila

Rosalind continued to care for her mother. This must have been quite difficult as Margot became very demanding. As an example, Rosalind used to tell how she would come home from a difficult day's teaching, then, at her mother's insistence, shape the butter into delicate butter-pats for the evening meal. In 1932 she wrote to Janet to ask her if she could return from Australia to share the burden. Before the letter could be sent, however, news came of Janet's marriage to Tom Mason, so Rosalind was left to carry on alone – but not for much longer. Margot died in the Woolwich War Memorial Hospital at Greenwich in November, 1933, the same year the letters quoted above were written, and six years after Henry's death. She had developed a bad heart, and died when she suffered a thrombosis after a goitre operation. She was buried in the churchyard at Winchelsea alongside Henry. Extraordinarily, in her will she left £1355. I can't account for that seemingly large amount. The beneficiaries were the two children who had been close by – Christopher and Rosalind.

CHAPTER 5

What of the other members of my mother's family in England? Before continuing the Australian story, we should pick up the unfinished threads there.

First, Aunt Anna. We've mentioned the death of my mother's parents, Henry and Margot Hazard, in 1927 and 1933, respectively. Henry's sister, Anna – who married Bernard Barton – lived on for a long time. My mother sent her food parcels during and after the war. She was very grateful, though she replied, "I am only sorry that you were under the impression that we were short of food. I'm afraid that this is very serious on the Continent, & it is perfectly marvellous that here we do not suffer in this way." I think many people *were* suffering, but Aunt Anna was comfortably placed. She died in 1944, aged eighty-eight, leaving my mother a sizeable amount of money. We had been living at Winston for some four or five years. Mum determined to spend the money on building two rooms (they were always called dormitories) and an attached bathroom beside the house. It had always been a romantic idea of Mum's that she could have a place for children to come and stay. This would be a boon for the children, and would bring in some income, as well. There was fierce opposition to this. Dad was silent and stubborn. Opinion amongst us children was divided. Against this background, Mum went ahead. Dick James and his brother-in-law, Charlie Rowlerson, came and built the dormitories, and children began to arrive. They were almost entirely from Melbourne, and came in the school holidays.

However there were very few of them. I suppose that over the course of five or six years only a couple of dozen children came to stay, and that includes multiple visits by some of them. Mum once answered an appeal in a women's magazine from 'Desperate' for somewhere to stay. She came, with her small daughter, and was there for a couple of months. I don't think she paid anything. It wasn't a success. There was a social divide, I think we could say. All in all, Aunt Anna's money slipped away.

* * *

Next we come to my grandmother's family, the Tooths, and trace their descendants. Of the eight children in the Tooth family – my grandmother, Margot, and her brothers and sisters– seven married, but of those only four had children, and with three of those four the line seems destined to be short-lived.

The first of those three was Margot herself - Margot who married Henry Hazard and had seven children. We've heard about that family – *our* family – in some detail. They're the ones who have continued to flourish.

The second in the Tooth family to marry and have offspring was Edwin, who married Mabel Barnes. I actually met Mabel at Oundle in 1964 when Waltheof, Philippa, and Christopher brought her for afternoon tea. She is the only one of that generation of Tooths – or Hazards - I ever met. Edwin and Mabel had one child, Waltheof, you remember. His full name was Waltheof Edwin Shepperson Tooth. The name Shepperson comes from a forebear on the Barnes side who was a painter of some repute in the early nineteenth century. Waltheof became a solicitor with Collissons and Dawes in London, and married Philippa Scott, who was related to Captain Oates, a member of Scott's ill-fated South Pole adventure. Waltheof served in the Middle East during the War. It remained the great adventure of his life and he wrote some very entertaining memoirs of his experiences. Again, Waltheof and Philippa had one child, Christopher. They lived in inner-west London, in Richmond and East Sheen, Philippa into her eighties and Waltheof into his nineties. Philippa was very involved with the Samaritans. They were a very cultivated couple. Anne and I had dinner with them in Richmond in 1991. Waltheof was full of mirth. I will always remember how he could put on the most marvellous Norfolk accent and tell funny stories in that voice. I have some of them on tape. His own voice was distinctly 'proper'. On the walls of the sitting-room were hanging the paintings of his forebear, Matthew Shepperson, which he showed us with great pride. Philippa had an interesting life, having been born in India, educated in England, and working as a nurse in England and South Africa before marrying Waltheof. Christopher is unmarried. He worked for some time with Virgin Records, in their classical music department, before setting up on his own in the same field. To bring Christopher's story up to date, I have to leap forward to 2011! Things were going badly for Christopher. His business was on its beam ends. He decided to sell several of the paintings his father had left him, the very ones we had seen hanging in Waltheof's sitting room in Richmond twenty years earlier. They were expected to fetch a couple of hundred pounds each. Christopher took them to the auction house, Bonham's. There, one of the paintings - which they entitled 'Portrait of a Gentleman' - caught their eye. They sent it for expert analysis. It turned out to be not by Shepperson but by the Spanish master, Velazquez, and fetched a fortune when eventually auctioned. Christopher and his cousin Rachael are our two remaining family connections in England.

The third of the Tooths to marry and have children was Olive, who married Edmund Candler. Audrey and Kit were the children. Kit married Dorothy Few. They had no children and lived in South Africa. As we've heard, Audrey married Bill McGeagh, and Rachael is their daughter. After Bill's death, Audrey lived out her life in Tangier. We met her in England once, and again when she came to Sydney while on a cruise in the late 'sixties. Rachael has led a very interesting life. When she was two, her father was appointed to a Colonial Office position in Kenya, and Rachael was there until she was six. Rachael remembers bumping along in a string hammock with a runner at each end while her father was on safari collecting taxes, her father and mother walking beside her. While her parents stayed in Kenya, Rachael came to England, to a succession of homes with friends and relatives and a succession of wonderful schools in Scotland, Buckinghamshire, and Norfolk. By 1939, when the war began, Rachael's father held an appointment in Palestine. Rachael had some time at a school in Jerusalem run by the Sisters of Sion, then managed to get back to England with her mother while her father remained in Jerusalem. She joined the WRNS and served for several years. Then followed a time, after the war, as secretary to her father in Palestine, now District Commissioner in Gaza. She was there at the time of the terrorist bombing of the King David Hotel and helped her father salvage secret documents from the wreckage. Rachael then developed TB and spent two and a half years in treatment in England and a sanatorium in Switzerland. After a brief unsuccessful marriage, she entered the law as an articled clerk, which was the beginning of a long career as a solicitor in London. Rachael has become a close friend of the Connelly family. Several of us have stayed with her in England and she has visited us in Australia. She has contributed enormously to this history. Rachael now lives in Halesworth in Suffolk, close to the old heartland of the Hazards and Tooths.

The fourth of the Tooth family to produce family was Wilfred who lived in Canada and married Florence. Their son, Max, died in a flying accident, though Florence married again after Wilfred's death and had a daughter, Lily. They have passed completely beyond our ken.

CHAPTER 6

We continue to jump from one generation to another. We have just completed the coverage of Margot Hazard's family, the Tooths. Now we come to her children, the seven Hazards of Harleston. We heard earlier about Noel, Val, and Charlie, who all died young, although I need to add something to what my mother wrote about Charlie and his involvement in the Great War. The truth is hard to determine. Some say he spent some months serving in Ireland, and that he had a very hard time and returned broken in body and spirit. Others say that it was arranged by some person in authority that he would serve as a despatch rider in France, where he would be out of danger, but in fact, either through error or through urgency, he was placed in the front line, and, again, was completely overwhelmed. Searching British war records brings no clear solution to the problem. His name does not come up in the lists of serving personnel where Noel's and Val's do. There are some teasing possibilities. A 'C Hazzard' enlisted in the Royal Marines Light Infantry in August, 1917 and was discharged five weeks later as "irregularly enlisted". There are all the earmarks of this man being Charles, except that his birth date was 31 May, 1898, completely wrong for Charles. Could it be a clerical error? Our Aunt Rosalind was quite firm that Charles had enlisted. Was she thinking of his service in his school cadets? Late in her life she was confused about where he was buried. Was she similarly confused about his war service? I believe that it remains doubtful that he served in the war. Perhaps he tried to enlist and was rejected. Years later, Charlie contracted TB while at the hospital in Thorpe. He received virtually no treatment, and died there when he was thirty-two. Charlie is buried at Redenhall St Mary.

There were four others – Janet, Joyce, Christopher, and Rosalind. The oldest of these was Janet Mary Marguerite, familiarly and lovingly known in our family as Aunty Janet. Her birth and baptism were recorded by her father, as were the others', in his formal (and superstitious?) manner:

> *Memorandum as to the Family Records of Wm. Hy. Hazard & M. Hazard … Their 3rd. Child, Janet Mary Marguerite was born at Harrolds on Monday, 28th Nov., 1898 at 11.10 o'clock a.m. 1st Monday in Advent & 6 hours after the full moon & was christened at S. Mary's Church Pulham by the Rev. C.C. Wakefield on Wednesday, 28th December follg, Holy Innocents Day at 12.30 o'clock noon. Present Rev. F.C. Hibberd, Mrs. Edith Morley Smith, sponsors, & Miss Elizth Candler, proxy for Miss Mary O'Brien.*

Janet was at school at Saint Felix, Southwold, from age fourteen to sixteen. Her sister, my mother, Joyce, started there with her. Their father took a house, 'Hillside,' in Southwold, where the girls lived, presumably under adult care, and they attended the school as day-girls. Janet went on to Swanley, a horticultural college near Sevenoaks in Kent, which at this time admitted only women students. When the Princess Royal married Viscount Lascelles in Westminster Abbey in 1922, William Henry and Margot Hazard, together with their eldest daughter

"Miss Hazard" (Janet) were invited to the wedding because of the family connection my mother spoke of earlier. However they had to refuse the invitation because they could not afford to buy the clothes that would be necessary. In 1924, when she was twenty-five, Janet came to Australia, never to return. It's always been believed that she was sent out by her parents to check on my mother. Janet had brought from England letters of introduction from some quite influential people, but she destroyed them. She had many jobs, mostly in the country. At one time she worked in a clothing factory. At another time she was working as a teacher's aide at Whittlesea in Victoria. Janet had a yen to help others. This took her at one time to a farming family near Mildura who were on their uppers, where she helped, with no pay, to look after the children. On two occasions, Janet worked on a big station at Jerilderie in New South Wales as a shearers' cook. She enjoyed this very much. There she met one of the station-hands, a fellow-Englishman, Tom Mason. Janet and Tom were married at the Church of England in Creswick in 1932, and moved into the place our family had just vacated. To begin with Tom had a vegetable round. He would buy vegetables in Ballarat and take them round Creswick, but it didn't succeed. The Depression was a bad time for this kind of work. Tom went on to work on the land and for many years as a ship's stoker. Their first child, Noel, was born in 1933. Rosalind, Marguerite (Margot), and Clem followed. Rosalind was born on 29th February, 1936, so enjoys a birthday every four years! By the time of the Second World War, the Masons were living in St Albans, a suburb of Melbourne. They moved to Nar Nar Goon in Gippsland, then to Garfield, first in 'Trasler's house' on the 13-Mile Road, then in

Mont Albert Road for several years. Here, Janet received some money in Aunt Anna's will, just as my mother did, and with that she bought a house and some land at Longwarry North, where Janet was able to fulfil her long-held desire to farm the land. She called the place, 'Waveney'. I remember visiting her there when she was cultivating garden crops using a small, hand-held petrol-driven rotary hoe. Eventually, Tom and Janet moved back to Melbourne, to Greensborough. After Tom's death, Janet lived with Rosalind and Heinz in Ashburton. She died in 1984.

Of the Mason children, Noel became a successful business man, and was well-known as an expert industrial valuer with his own auctioneering business. He was married first to Joan Babbage. The children are Robbyn and Christopher. After that marriage failed, Noel married Susan Collins, and their son is Alexander. Noel died in 2013. Rosalind became a primary-school teacher, and travelled to Africa and England where she met some of her Hazard and Tooth relations. Rosalind married Heinz Gross, who came to Australia after a very difficult time in Europe during and after the War. They are now retired, living in Melbourne. Margot was also a teacher. She married Ron Masters, a builder. Soon after their marriage they moved to Sydney and then to Wagga Wagga in New South Wales. Their children are Jennifer and Janet. Clem married Aileen Goldsworthy. Their children are Dean and Garry. Clem was married again to Marion Bertoulli. Clem was in the trucking industry. Sadly, in 1999, he died in an accident as he vainly attempted to stop a runaway truck. The family tree for the Mason family, at Rosalind's request, is not completed in detail.

* * *

Leaving out my mother, next in the family came Christopher. He loomed large in our family at Garfield, though only one of us children ever met him – Angela, who was his god-daughter. After leaving Oundle (where he seems to have made little impact; the only record of him there is that he was run out for 3 in a house cricket match!), he studied at Cambridge, but didn't do well. In fact he had a bigger reputation as a debtor than as a scholar. He even fell foul of his own family in his efforts to clear his debts. He cut short his time at Cambridge and set out on a teaching career. In 1933, I know, he was at Winton House Preparatory School in Winchester, where he drove a fast car when he was able to get away from the classroom. Then he joined up. During the war, say in 1943, we started a 'Winston Journal,' at Garfield after the style of our Uncle Val's 'Caltofts Courier,' and Christopher sent a contribution for it. All issues of the Winston Journal have been lost, but I can remember the opening lines of Christopher's poem:

> *I'd love to see a kangaroo*
> *come bounding through*
> *the eucalyptus blue.*

It's the improbable scansion that made it stick in my mind! Christopher served as an officer in the British Army during the war. All I know about that is that he took part in the Burma campaign, where at one time he was in charge of a donkey transport unit. He was very impressed by the good nature of his West African troops, and that influenced him in going to Africa when the war was over. In 1947, he bought a Preparatory School - Pembroke House – at Gil Gil in Kenya, 120 kilometres north of Nairobi. It covered 110 acres in a beautiful setting, five kilometres from Gil Gil itself, 2,000 metres above sea level, and on the edge of the Rift Valley. Besides owning it, he was also the Headmaster, although over the course of his eighteen years of running the school, ownership was transferred to a Charitable Trust.

Now it's time to tell one of our favourite family stories. Soon after he began at Pembroke, Christopher found he had need of a matron. He thought of an old friend, Alfreda Johns (her full name was Alfreda Gough Johns), who had been at Swanley with Aunty Janet, and used to visit Caltofts in the old days. He wrote home to her, explaining his need and ending with words like this: "Would you come and join me here?" Alfreda interpreted this as a marriage proposal, consulted one or two friends who agreed with her, and arrived at Gil Gil with her trousseau. Christopher was too much of a gentleman to let her down, and so it was that she became our Aunt Alfreda. This account comes from Alfreda and Christopher themselves. It is one of the best-loved stories in the family repertoire and is set in concrete. Now, it is sad to destroy a family legend so thoroughly accepted and so often repeated. However the marriage records of Great Britain show that Christopher Martin Hazard married Alfreda Gough Johns in Alfreda's home town of Cardiff, Glamorgan in 1942. Was the wedding kept secret? For reasons of Alfreda's employment? Did Christopher invent the other story and perpetuate the myth? Or was Alfreda responsible? If so, for what reason? Was there a separation after 1942 and a reconciliation in 1947? Or even a divorce and re-marriage? Will we ever know?

Pembroke House was a Boarding School preparing the sons of settlers for the British Public Schools, although the school has since become co-educational. Christopher Hazard was an extraordinary headmaster. He gave all he had to the school. Old Boys write of Christopher in the most affectionate terms. "It was not long," one wrote, "before everyone appreciated that he was most definitely a 'character' or even an eccentric." He was known to the boys as 'Quelch'. Finding difficulties in transporting boys to other schools for games, he bought a 1914 Rolls-Royce tourer and had it cut down to make a passenger vehicle for twelve boys – a cricket team! He had the boys build a pigeon loft. When a team was playing away, they took some pigeons with them. At half-time, the score was sent home via a pigeon, and likewise at the end of a game. The result would be known by the time the team returned. Christopher had a swimming pool built and made every boy learn to swim. He established model railways for the boys. The school ran a pack of basset hounds with which the boys would go shooting, which was one of Uncle Christopher's chief joys.

But the crowning glory of his time at the school was the building of a chapel, known as the Christina Chapel. Officially, it was named after the mother of the Head Boy who laid the foundation stone (on Coronation Day, 1953), but we in the family know better – that it was named for Alfreda's mother, Christina Johns. Alfreda's oldest sister was also Christina. To discover the size needed, Christopher had all the boys sit on the grass in rows and drew a line around them. That's where the walls went. Christopher was the architect and overseer, but the boys did everything – digging the foundations, making the mud bricks, mixing the cement, drilling and riveting the roof girders, making the stained-glass windows. The coloured glass for the windows was from broken glass, the blue coming from milk-of-magnesia bottles. Lead to hold the glass in place was from old toothpaste tubes and car batteries. My cousin, Rosalind Mason, while she was staying at Pembroke, did the sketch of St George and the Dragon for the feature window. The building took eight years to construct. Alfreda was active in school affairs. "Not a sparrow fell without her knowledge and concern," according to an old boy. He went on, "... she knew more about the parents and home-life of the boys than most of the parents. What a blockbuster of a book she could have written."

From 1952 to 1956, the Mau Mau rebellion occurred. This was a difficult time for staff and students. The school's isolation was a huge concern. It was surrounded by barbed wire, flood-lit at night, and protected by armed guards. Fortunately no problems occurred, although we've always believed that Christopher's good relations with the local African people was a reason for that. After Kenya became an independent republic, the school began to admit African students, although few attended because of the relatively high fees. In 1965, Christopher was struck down by a serious heart attack, and had to give up the headmastership immediately. He was broke. He had put all his resources into the school without stint. Parents and friends raised a large sum through a testimonial appeal. Christopher

Christopher Martin Hazard at Pembroke House

and Alfreda were given a house to live in on the property of a school family ten miles from Nanyuki, with a wonderful view of Mount Kenya. Christopher lived out his life here with Alfreda, their Labrador, 'Brock', several black servants, and many 'English' friends round about. My sister, Angela, and her husband, Ewen, visited them in 1976. Angela wrote back that Christopher was "an absolute pet, a man of very few words, an absolute gentleman, very ill and slow now, the driest wit, and altogether perfect." Christopher died the next year. Alfreda then went to Canada to be with her brother, but soon returned to England and died in 1983 at Rush Court, 'a home for gentlewomen' at Wallingford in Oxfordshire. Anne and I visited Pembroke House in 2005, and talked to staff members who remembered Christopher very fondly. One of the school parents said of him, "I have known no one more genuine or with greater integrity. All of us consider ourselves fortunate indeed to have had the Hazards at Pembroke over those vital years."

Placing the walls for the Christina Chapel. The tall figure of Uncle Christopher in rear

There is one story about Uncle Christopher that has never been recorded, but is part of our family lore. On the eve of April Fools Day one year, while Headmaster, remember, he went round the dormitories as the boys slept, and painted a purple 'moustache' on the upper lip of each boy. They woke to find themselves victims of, surely, one of the greatest April Fools Day pranks ever!

* * *

To go back, now, to Rosalind. She was with her parents when they were forced out of Caltofts in 1925, and later trained as a teacher at Avery Hill College in Eltham, London. She taught at Limpsfield Church of England Village School in Surrey (which is still going strong) and later at Horley, also in Surrey, where she boarded with Madeline Agar, who was one of the first women landscape gardeners in England. Madeline had taught Janet at Swanley and became a good friend of Rosalind's for the next forty years. (Madeline Agar's brother, Wilfrid Agar, was Professor of Zoology at Melbourne University for thirty years, and taught Tessy there in the 1940s). Rosalind remained in teaching until the outbreak of war in 1939, when she enlisted in the Women's Land Army. She was thoroughly happy in her work there. Rosalind was the keeper of the documents of the Hazard family history, and on her death they came to me. They were contained in the 'Bible Box,' an oak chest of some antiquity, which was sent out to Australia by Rachael following Rosalind's death. Rosalind's own life may be charted in part from some of her personal books that came in the Bible Box. One of these is a Prayer Book which is well-worn despite

Rosalind's assertion that she forswore religion in 1932, at the time of Charlie's death. The Prayer Book is carefully inscribed by Rosalind with her full name and the date, 17 January, 1914 - her eighth birthday. Then there is a gift from her father for her eighteenth birthday. This is Thomas A Kempis', 'The Imitation of Christ', and is inscribed in his strong hand, 'R.A Hazard, 17 Jan, 1924. WHH.' The choice of book and the severe wording of the inscription indicate something of William Henry Hazard's nature. The third book comes from Rosalind's time in the Women's Land Army. After a posting at Hinckley in Leicestershire, Rosalind was put in charge of a hostel for Land Army girls at Idlicote in Warwickshire. The book is unimportant in itself, being a portrait of Tewkesbury in the early twentieth century. The inscription reads, "To Miss Hazard, from all the girls at Idlicote Hostel, Christmas, 1945," and there follows a list of forty-four signatures. One of those girls, sixty years later, described her time there, and through her, we can glimpse something of Rosalind's concerns.

> The work was pretty much the same, dusty, dirty threshing. When we meet now we always wonder why we haven't had T.B. or something from the dust. We wore apart from dungarees etc. three scarves, one tied like a turban and one around our necks then one on our heads and tied under our chins. These were not really scarves, but 6d first aid arm slings from Boots. Occasionally we tied strings round our trouser legs near the bottom if we were not wearing gum boots to stop the mice and rats running up our legs! Can you imagine city girls going through this but we soon got used to it. Sometimes we worked with

animals which was a bright start to a day. I worked with cows which I loved, and cart horses.

Rosalind made good friends, one of the closest being Barbara Price. They would often go away together, once, in the early thirties, on a walking tour of Normandy. During those years, Rosalind spent a lot of time caring for her mother until Margot died in 1933. Rosalind was now free to visit us all in Australia, and did so the following year, 1934. I was too young to remember her coming, but she brought us an elephant made from teak, which I still have.

When the war ended, Rosalind taught for a year or two in a Men's Teacher Training College in Nottinghamshire, and then bought a lovely 18th-century house at Clifton-on-Teme, high in the hills above Worcester. This was 'Oak House', a quaint old timber-framed cottage in the main street. The date, '1721' was carved on the doorhead, but there were some alterations over the next century. There was a narrow, twisting staircase to get upstairs, and three dormer windows looking into the street. Rosalind ran it as a tea-house, with the assistance of two notable companions, Mrs Ford and Bunty. This is where my family and I spent Christmas in 1962 and 1963, deep in snow, and where my mother spent many months while she was in England at the same time. Rosalind was a very independent person, with quite fixed views, and I think there were some difficult moments during that time.

Rosalind came out to Australia twice more, once in the late sixties and once in the late seventies. On her first visit, I was teaching at Cranbrook, and had the honour of taking her and her two sisters, my mother and Aunty Janet, to the School, the home of their grandfather, Robert Tooth, and where their mother had almost certainly lived, at least for a short time, as a baby. There they signed the official Visitors' Book. On Rosalind's second visit, we were living at Portland. I remember one famous evening when we took her out to the Melaleuca Restaurant for dinner. Rosalind almost exploded when she found 'Melaleuca Special' on the dessert menu – plum pudding dipped in batter and deep-fried!

With Oak House proving too much for her, Rosalind moved to a unit in a small retirement complex in Ely, 'St Mary's Court', in the grounds of St Mary's Church, and only a few hundred metres from Ely Cathedral. She was very happy there. She studied jewellery-making and was a keen member of the Liberal Party. She died in 1987, and I interred her ashes in the grounds of St Mary's Court in 1991. My wife, Anne, and Rachael were with me, and Ivy, one of Rosalind's friends from the Court. She left a sizeable sum to each of her nieces and nephews in her will - and some money to Mother Teresa.

CHAPTER 7

Meanwhile, on Dad's side, the ranks of his parents' generation were thinning also. His parents, as you know, had died even before the First War. Within a few years of the war ending, he had lost his grandparents on both the Connelly and the Curran sides.

To pick up the loose ends, I'll go back first to the generation of Connellys next above my father, the children of the original two, James Connelly and Catherine O'Neil, and add anything I can to what my father has already said. There were nine of them, remember - William, Jim, Maggie, Pat, Tim, Michael, Richard, Mary Ann, and Catherine.

My father didn't want to say much about his own father, William, the first of that family. That's probably because there wasn't much good to say about him. He used to spend a lot of his money betting on racehorses and got very little of it back. And he drank too much. He died in 1909 after falling into Lake Wendouree. I don't know the details, but many people have put two and two together. His wife, Cecilia, my grandmother, had died the previous year.

Dad has already said quite a bit about his uncle Jim, who was next in the family – how he went to Western Australia and came back only the once. I can't add anything to that, except that a James Connelly died in Perth in 1925, and I think that was him. He would have been sixty.

The next two in the family were Maggie and Pat. Everybody always thinks of them together. Neither of them married, and they were the ones who stayed on at the old Connelly place in Weatherboard and kept the family together. As Dad indicated, they were shrewd in their dealings and acquired more land over time. Pat inherited the farm in his father's will, and quite a large amount in cash. Pat died in 1937, and the place was sold. Maggie moved to Waubra, about ten kilometres away, to live with her niece, Annie, and her husband, Bill Gallagher. Maggie was there in Waubra for many years, until she died at the age of eighty-two. She and Pat, fittingly, are buried together in Learmonth Cemetery. The inscription on their gravestone is moving in its understated way:

>*In Loving Memory of*
>*My Dear Brother*
>*PATRICK CONNELLY*
>*Died 9th February, 1937*
>*Aged 67 years*
>
>*His loved sister*
>*MARGARET CONNELLY*
>*Died 4th April, 1950*
>*Aged 82 years*

My dad also told us quite a lot about his Uncle Tim, the orator. He was seventy-two when he died in 1943. He's buried at Learmonth, but away from the others. He'd held himself at somewhat of a distance in life. So too, in death, he lies apart.

But he was not alone for long. Five years later, Tim's nephew, Ted Hannabry, was buried with him, both of them single men. Ted's mother was Tim's little sister, Catherine. Tim had looked after Ted over the years.

Next came Michael. We've already heard how he died in his early thirties.

There's more to say about Richard Thomas, the next in line. You'll know from what my father said that Richard and his wife, Lil, had three children – Kathleen, Vincent and Richard. To take them in reverse order, Richard was killed in the Second World War, aged nineteen. Vincent married Ada (Anne) Richards; they had a daughter, Cheryl. Kath married Bob Elliot. Kath had her Uncle Jim's prayer book (the one who went to Western Australia). Their three children, Denise, Patricia, and Robyn, all married and had families. This family is one of the few who carried on the line, and so provided us with some cousins. Of the nine children born to the original James and Catherine Connelly, six died without issue.

The eighth in that family was Mary Ann, who died as a baby.

The last was Catherine, who, to make up for the others, was very prolific. She married Jim Hannabry, as my father told us. The first of her six children was Maggie, who married Pat Ryan, and farmed with him at Waubra. During the early 1940s, we Connelly children went on holiday to Aunt Maggie's farm once or twice, and Maggie and Pat's oldest child, Patricia, once came to stay with us at Garfield. Noel and I have memories of playing in the hay at Waubra in a huge hay-shed with the Ryan children. There were five of them - Patricia, Desmond, Margaret, Mary, and Verna. Patricia married Tom Troy, though she is now widowed and lives in Ballarat; Desmond farmed near Waubra; Margaret married Bill Murphy and moved to Geelong; Mary married Jim Flynn and went to Kyneton; and Verna married Graham Loader, a farmer from Burrumbeet. Catherine Hannabry's second child was Mary. Mary married Bill McMahon. There were three children, Billy, Kevin, and Carmel. In her old age Mary lived in Croydon. Anne and I visited her there and listened to her stories about the family in days gone by. She was wonderfully friendly and helpful. She was born in the first years of the twentieth century, so could reach back into very early days of the family's history. Her memory was very acute, and a lot of what's written here is based on what she told us – our only shaft of light into that period gone by. As for the other four of Catherine's family – Ted, Alice, Kathleen, and Jack - I don't know any more about them apart from what my father has written.

* * *

My dad left quite a few things hanging in the air. For the sake of thoroughness (but at the risk of over-supplying the detail) I need to follow through with Dad's own family – his brothers and sisters. He's already told us of Jim and Ben and Cissie, all of whom died young. The other four were Annie, Patsy, Johnnie, and Catherine.

As Dad said, his sister Annie married Bill Gallagher and moved with him to Waubra. I believe there were seven children. One - Mary - died aged only eleven. Another, Cecilia, married Harry Harrison from Waubra, and they had nine children. Annie lived many years as a widow, dying in 1970.

Dad's brother Patsy – Patrick Thomas Connelly - remains a mystery man. He made the break from Weatherboard about the time of the Second World War, and never contacted his family again. My sister Tessy, when at university in the 'forties, tried to trace him. She knocked on the door of a house in Williamstown where she thought he might live. A man of the right vintage appeared and closed the door as soon as she spoke of her quest. On the other hand, there was a man of his name and age who died in Lara in 1968. Perhaps that was him.

Johnnie was the second youngest in Dad's own family. He lived for some time at Waubra with Aunty Kate Curran, who had reared him and who later bought a little house there at Waubra. When his Aunty Kate died, Johnnie went into Ballarat and lived with the Loreto nuns at the convent. One of his relatives, Sr Gerard Briody was there at the time. (Aunty Kate Curran's brother, Jack, had married a Briody from Lexton). He lived in a hut alongside the Convent, working in the vegetable garden along with Jimmy who was deaf. Johnnie was shy to the point of being a recluse, but quite clever. He wrote and painted and did crossword puzzles. Eventually Johnnie's health deteriorated and he died in 1970.

Finally, there was Dad's youngest sister, Catherine. Catherine Agnes, known as Katie. My father mentioned how she contracted hydatids and was never well. Katie was cared for by Maggie and Pat Ryan in Waubra (Maggie was her cousin), and died in Ballarat in 1939, when she was thirty-four. She is buried in the Learmonth Cemetery.

It's rather sad that the wider family relations – 'our sisters and our cousins and our aunts' – have drifted out of contact. There must be quite a few of them, stemming from the Currans, as well as from Richard Thomas Connelly, and Catherine Hannabry. Also, it's possible that the missing Patsy might have married and had children.

CHAPTER 8

In 1935 began my family's long association with Garfield. Twenty-two years later, in 1957, when my parents sold up and moved to Carrum in Melbourne, my mother was presented with a handsome mantel clock 'as a token of esteem by St. Mary's Guild and Garfield friends'. Each member of the family made their mark on the town in different ways, but it was my mother who was known and respected most widely.

For a short time we were in a very small house in Brownbill Road, a kilometre or two south of the town, on the Koo Wee Rup Swamp, by now drained and cleared, but still known as 'The Swamp.' Just weeks before our arrival there had been a monster flood which inundated all the land around us. Our landlady was a Mrs Dickson or Dixon, who was at first regarded as something of an ogre, but who proved to be quite the opposite. A hill nearby was known as Governor's Hill, because the Governor of Victoria in the 1880s, Sir Henry Lock, came here duck-shooting in the time before the swamps were drained. On this hill, standing out above the surrounding flats, the Pratts had their farm. They were to become our good friends. We got to know the Traslers who lived on the 13-Mile Road nearby. Harold Trasler was an ex-World War 1 man, like Dad. So was Percy Pratt. Further along the 13-Mile Road lived a large Irish family. They were very poor and eventually burnt their house down for the insurance. Fortunately, all their bedding was on the clothes-line at the time, and much of the furniture moved out of doors to be cleaned! This was a great joke in our family.

Dad was digging potatoes, and although he travelled some distance – to Neerim, for instance – that didn't occupy him for the whole year. The Depression was still very severe. The government introduced a scheme where unemployed men would be given work on projects such as road maintenance in exchange for a small living wage. This was known as sustenance work, but always referred to as 'susso'. Payment was made at the rate of 8/6 (eight shillings and sixpence) a week for a married man, with an additional 1/6 for each child. In addition, the men were provided with an identification card which enabled them to receive groceries, meat, bread, and milk. They could also get clothing and footwear for children, firewood, and rental assistance. Dad was on susso at various periods in the late thirties. I can remember him clearing roadside drains in Garfield. That must have been 1938 or 1939. I remember particularly because while I was there he disturbed a snake in the drain and killed it with his shovel while I watched. Afterwards we walked home together, Dad wheeling his bike.

* * *

In 1936, we moved to another rented house in Archer Road in Garfield, but which we knew as Slaughterhouse Road. The slaughterhouse and paddocks were across the road from our house, although they didn't impinge on us at all, except that we'd play there and find jaw-bones we'd use as pistols. This house was always known as Webbs'. I presume we rented it from a Mr Webb, although I don't remember him ever materialising. This is where I came to years of remembrance. The Orlandis, Italian immigrants, were our closest neighbours, not friends, though we used to knock about with the two children. Another Italian family lived further up our road – the Cafisos. Mary Cafiso was the same age as I was and my good friend. Some time later the Cafisos' house burnt down. There was a sports meeting in progress at the football ground (was it New Year's Day?), and we were all there when we saw the black smoke rising. An announcement came over the loudspeaker telling all nearby residents they should return home. Mrs Cafiso was missing and it was feared she had been caught in the house, but Tessy found her along the road, sitting on the bank and crying. It turned out she had lost a lot of very beautiful needlework she had brought out from Italy. The Cafisos moved away and we never heard of them again. Around the corner and up the hill lived the two sisters, the Miss McKays, Annie and Margaret. They had the milk round in Garfield. I can't think where they got the milk from, but they took it round the town with their horse and jinker, ladling the various quantities into the jugs people would leave outside their doors. When they died many years later, their nephew, Hec Wikman, found thousands of pounds stashed behind their stove.

*   *   *

We must have been in Webbs' only a couple of years, because in 1938 we moved into another house owned, this time, by Mr Barker. The house was small and old – and hot! I remember us trying to sleep, lying out on the grass on some summer nights because it was too hot in the house. The back entrance porch had an earthen floor. The kitchen was the centre of activity. Each morning my mother would rise early and scrape out the previous night's ashes and kindle the new fire. I would wake to the delicious smell of smoke and the sound of the scraping and snapping of sticks and the opening and closing of the fire-box as the flame was coaxed into life. This early-morning ritual became a token of security for me in my dozy comfortableness, especially when the smells of toast and frying eggs might also reach me through the open door.

There were thirty acres attached to the house, although it was mostly bushland. We did have a house cow, however, called Darkie. I remember the cowshed more than the cow, because, in the most daring moment of my life to that stage, I followed Noel in jumping off the cowshed roof on to the ground. Soon I was doing it all the time! I don't know who Mr Barker was, though I do know he also owned Parish's place – their house and orchard. He also owned some land across the road where he grew potatoes one year. He hired Noel to pick up potatoes behind the diggers and paid him six shillings a day. In January 1939, we stood down near the road and watched a bushfire spotting near us, on this same land. Cinders were falling around us and we beat them out as they landed. This was January the thirteenth, Black Friday, when fires swept through the State and seventy people lost their lives. Noojee was wiped out. We talked a lot about Noojee being burnt because Dad had been up that way digging potatoes and knew some of the people who were affected.

By now, Dad had got a job with the Forestry Commission. He remained there for the rest of his working life, until he was sixty-four. That means he was there for almost twenty years. He was away all week. On Monday morning, early, in the dark in winter, he would pack his supplies for the week – corned beef, potatoes, bread, sugar and tea - in a sugar bag, sling it over his shoulder, and walk down into Garfield, where he was picked up by Sam McDonald or his boss, Tim Warren, and driven to the camp at Gentle Annie, one of the higher peaks in the Black Snake Range, north of Longwarry. His work was to keep the road and phone lines clear, check the timber trucks bringing out logs, writing down the measurements so that the correct amount of royalty could be paid, and, in summer, keeping a lookout from the tower on the top of the mountain for bushfires. The bearings of fires would be radioed through to Neerim South, where they would be cross-checked with other reports to find the precise location of the fire. It was responsible work, and he was very good at it. His accommodation was a hut. Some boxes served as furniture, and his bed consisted of potato bags stitched together and slung from bush-timber supports. There was a communal drop-toilet. The radio and other paraphernalia were housed in a timber shed. Two or three men lived and worked there, each in their own hut. Alongside the huts was a large dug-out, where the men could take shelter in the event of bushfire. Noel and I, separately, would sometimes go and camp there with Dad for a week in the school holidays. I remember the earthy smell of the bush and the silence of the great forests. On Friday night, Dad would reappear at home, through the bottom gate and along the track to the house. When I was young, I would run to meet him. As I write this down, Dad's life in the bush sounds like a miserable existence, but I think he was content. He liked the routine; he was free from other obligations; the foibles of his companions and the small incidents of his daily work occupied his mind and provided material for dinner-table anecdotes at home.

This house – Barkers' - is always called *Lombardos'* in the family. The Lombardos followed us as tenants there. Mr Lombardo was the barber down the street, and I would sit on a wooden box on his chair while he cut my hair. I can't remember much about Mrs Lombardo, except that, in a moment of confusion she once poured boiling water from the kettle into the opened tea-packet instead of the teapot. In 1940, not long before we left Lombardos', Mum had to go to hospital in Melbourne for several weeks. I think it was to have a hysterectomy. Tessy was sent off to the Sturdys, Angela to the Larsens, and Noel and I to the Miss McKays, the milk-ladies. Mum kept the letters we wrote to her. Tessy's handwriting is clear and firm, her thoughts direct. She was thirteen.

> *Dear Mummy,*
>
> *I hope you didn't get much worse and are quite all right now. ... Last Sunday night Daddy came for tea and so did Myrtle and Alma Dawes and Keith Biddy. One day I was listening to the boys playing in bed; I heard Brian say, "Where have you been?" Ray: "New York." Brian: "What were you doing?" Ray: "Digging potatoes." Mr. Cox is a funny old man. He comes to tea some nights. One night when we were playing bobs, he wasn't doing much good. Our side had thirty-one to catch up and there was only him and me to have our shots. I was just going to have my turn, when he said, "You get thirty and leave me one."*

Does that sound funny to you? I have nearly finished seven skeins of my scarf – 3 more to knit. I have been knitting a skein a day. Next Friday is the Temperance physiology examination. I wonder how I'll get on this time. Angela didn't do too bad in her exams. Her average was at least a pass. ... Love from Tessy. [Lots of kisses and drawing of fairy and pixie included]

Angela, then twelve, wrote in her careful hand:

Dear Mummy,

I hope you got out of the After Care and got to Aunty Janet's all right. Thank you for your letter. ... For Jimmey's birthday, he got – From Daddy, scool cap with a footballer in front, a telephone and a little coloured torch. From Mrs. Pratt, a big tin of lollies. From Mrs. Sturdy, a beautiful, big pencil case. From Brian, a chocolate. From me, a water pistol. From Tessy, a coloured ball. That's all I know. I'm knitting a pair of mittins for the soldiers now. I've nearly got one finished just today. Old Charlie [the school bus driver, Charlie Styles] *got an abses in his ear, so he had to go home half way through the day. ... My abseses are better now and Tessy's eye hasn't a trace left. Well I suppose I had better close now. Goodbye. Love from ANGELA* [also lots of kisses].

Noel, aged nine, wrote in large characters in lead pencil:

> *Dear mum, I hope you are well. Dad writ to us yesterday. He told us you were at the after care hospital. We are very happy up here (I've only got a few lines to say). Were doing the milk round now. There is some new people moved into maybury's house. I dont know what they are called. Its only a little bit isent it. PTO* [drawing of horse and rails on back]

There is no letter from 'Jimmey' whose seventh birthday is mentioned above.

Who could have thought that these two – the boy who was "very happy up here" and the one who was too young to write – were, even as those letters were being written, engaged in one of the most daring escapades in the annals of primary school crime? The boys went off to school each day. The Miss McKays were busy. The Head Teacher was lax. False messages from other students were sent to him claiming illness. Each morning for three weeks, the two would set off for school, turn right instead of left at the main road, dart into the pine plantation, and emerge at their own house, abandoned through the week, with mother in hospital and father at work. There they would spend their day, exploring the bush, sometimes venturing as far as Mount Cannibal or the Main Drain (otherwise, the Bunyip River), eating their prepared lunch supplemented by potatoes from the kitchen roasted on an open fire, and generally poking their noses at authority in the manner of Butch Cassidy and the Sundance Kid. After three blissful weeks the law caught up with them. Summoned before their father, who stood sternly in front of the fireplace, the boys quailed in his presence. At least the younger one did. He was shortly dismissed. "I don't blame Jimmy," said Dad. "It's you," he said to Noel. What happened after I left I know not, but my brother was more subdued than was his wont for a long time afterwards.

The Connelly family at 'Lombardo's, 1939. Angela, Mum, Tessy, Jim, Noel. Tessy, uncharacteristically, is showing plenty of knee! Angela too! Dad absent, no doubt at work

The pine plantation immediately across the road was a place of wonder and secrecy. We spent long hours there. There was a warm, grassy corner near the main road from where we could spy on people and vehicles passing by. It was in that corner that Noel would give me my memory training. He'd set me a single word that I'd have to remember. Six months later he would ask me what it was, with attendant penalties for forgetfulness. But the most magical attraction beyond our own place was Mount Cannibal. This was a granite outcrop at North Garfield, standing out from the main range behind it, and about four kilometres from us. It can be seen for miles around. We would walk there,

'Lombardo's, Garfield, 1939. Touring party about to set off for Mount Cannibal. (l-r) Angela, Les James, June Salway, Jim, Tessy, Noel, Mum at back. Behind is the pine plantation across the road, scene of many nefarious activities

singly or on organised excursions, visitors often included, at least several times a year. We got to know each feature on the mountain intimately, especially the Cave, where the remains of aboriginal fires could be seen, at least in our imaginations, and, above all, the Precipice, a frightening rock-face on the southern peak, where Noel would terrify his mother by clambering dangerously close to the edge, and we would peer over to look for the skeletons of fallen victims. Getting to Mount Cannibal meant crossing the Princes Highway. We would wait for long periods for a vehicle to come along. The other children told me solemnly that Mrs Parish, who lived alongside the highway, had the job of cleaning the white line in the middle of the road. From the top of Mount Cannibal, above the Precipice, we could see our own house. If someone was at home, they would wave a white sheet and we could see it. That was a thrill. My mother wrote a beautiful poem about Mount Cannibal:

> *Down on the Highway the traffic is lumbering,*
> *Milk trucks and motor cars rattle and race:*
> *Watching eternally, silent, unslumbering,*
> *Hoary old Cannibal stands in his place.*
>
> *There in that place that is his since Creation,*
> *Earthquakes have rocked him and meteors caressed:*
> *Who can interpret that grand contemplation?*
> *Or fathom the secrets he holds in his breast?*
>
> *Why must our years pass in grief and in sorrow?*
> *In haste and in ferment, in terror of death?*
> *Now is Infinity, now and tomorrow:*
> *There, on the mountain, is God's very breath.*

CHAPTER 9

Behind our place at Lombardo's stood another farmlet of equal size – thirty acres - but with more than half the land cleared, and with a large and attractive house. Access to this place was along the track that ran beside our house. We would look across the fence at this place with envy. Miraculously, our dream became reality. Our friends, the Pratts, bought it for us. We knew them well through church – Mr and Mrs Pratt (Grace) and the three children of roughly our age, Jim, Nancy, and Tom. Mrs Pratt would send a Christmas parcel every year, with various delights for us children. She and Mum were particular friends. In 1940, they bought the place I've been speaking of, just for us. Perhaps there was a down-payment, and then we paid it off at the rate, I think, of five pounds a month, without interest. It must have been towards the end of the year that we moved in. I remember riding on the cart as Dad drove the first load of goods up there. Noel walked beside Captain, the horse. Mum and the girls had walked up earlier. As Noel opened the front gate we could see smoke coming from the chimney. "See that," said Dad, "It's your new home, boys." A rare moment of closeness and reflection.

We called it 'Winston' after the great war-time leader. It was our home for the next seventeen years, even long after we children individually left it. Indeed, if I had now to name a place that is my spiritual home, this would be it. In my mind, I walk over every inch, with perfect recall. What Caltofts was to my mother, Winston is to me. The house had an old section – our kitchen/dining room and a bedroom known as the Back Room, together with a crumbling open veranda, at one end of which was the bathroom. On to this original part had been built a small sitting room with an open fireplace, a huge drawing room, and another bedroom. There were two convenient corner verandas opening off these rooms. Noel and I slept in a sleep-out next to the house. There was no power connected to the house, so we used an 'Aladdin' pressure lamp as the main lighting source, with lanterns and candles to supplement it. All our schoolwork at night was done using these lights. Above the newer part of the house was a huge and high attic, which was a marvellous hideaway for us children because access to it was by climbing on to the roof of the kitchen and clambering through a small window, something which my mother couldn't do and my father wouldn't. The attic was unlined, and we walked about on the rafters, in fear of crashing through into the rooms below. There was no water supply, except for a thousand-gallon tank connected to the kitchen. When that ran out, we pumped water up from a well alongside.

* * *

It is the land, however, that I mostly dwell on. From the house, we looked out across the valley, past Parish's orchard, to the distant mountain range where Dad worked. We could name all the peaks – Walker's Ridge, Gentle Annie, North Gate, South Gate. The Front Paddock lay between the house and the front gate; behind the house was the Back Paddock; below the house was some open land that was never given a name, and below that the Middle Paddock. Alongside it was the Side Paddock, while the Bottom Paddock lay in the low land further away. Bracken fern and ti-tree were encroaching in some places. Tessy went out and with great determination chopped out fifteen bracken fern each day. Tessy was like that. There was open bush in three areas, on the sides of the property and at the very bottom. Dad and Noel chopped down trees for firewood, and we'd cart it home on a sledge drawn by the horse. We grew a crop every now and then in the Back Paddock or the Middle Paddock, where the best land lay – carrots once, maize another time, and potatoes once or twice. Dad would plough up the land with a single-furrow plough, though Noel became a master of ploughing also, and once single-handedly ploughed up the entire Middle Paddock for potatoes. I sometimes took the reins and drove the horse. "Come here!" we'd shout to steer left, "Gee off!" to steer right. Dad was in his element with this farm work, although he didn't let it show. We ran a couple of cows and had a draught horse, as well as a horse for us children to ride. There were kangaroos on the place, and snakes. It was there I killed my first snake. I was petrified of them, and probably with good reason, because we mostly went barefoot. My sense of achievement over my first snake was even greater than when I jumped off the cowshed roof.

Beside the house was a row of tall pine trees, which we boys would climb to the very top. In the yard, there was a store shed, which we called the feed shed. It had a gently-sloping roof, which was one of my favourite hideaways. Across from that was a two-storied hay shed, though it was mostly used for storage. This shed was known as Number Seven. The cart was stored there, and also a jinker, though I don't remember that being used. Around the perimeter of the yard area were the hen-houses, named, like the paddocks, with great logic but with little imagination, Number One and Number Two (these formed one building, divided in two sections), Numbers Three, Four, Five (again, one building, divided), and Number Six, which we built ourselves. The total number of chooks was three hundred. We sold the eggs to the Egg Board. T.J. Neylon's truck would come every Tuesday and pick them up, that is until the driver foolishly got his truck bogged in the Front Paddock, after which we had to cart the cases of eggs down to the main road half a kilometre away on a wheelbarrow. Because of the war, some of these eggs were destined for Britain, so we would have to preserve them before packing them in their cases. This was done by smearing the eggs with 'Ke-Peg'. My mother would mostly do this, at night, but we all helped at times. In fact, with Dad away all week, the chooks were Mum's responsibility, though we children did some of the work. Rats used to get under the nest-boxes, which were on the ground, so some Saturday mornings, led by Dad and with Mum noticeably absent, we'd have a rat hunt. With everyone in place holding their sticks, Dad would grab a row of boxes and fling them off, while we children flailed away at the fleeing rats, which seemed to be mostly babies.

We were often short of water for the cows. There was a small dam in the bush a long way from the house, but it was very inadequate and the water brackish. So Dad got Jack and Con Preston to come and sink a dam a hundred metres or so below the house. This was an exciting time, watching their horses and scoops biting into the ground, and later the water level inching upwards. When finished, it served as our swimming pool, even though the water was so muddy we couldn't see an inch below the surface. Jim Pratt built us a boat made from two sheets of roofing iron bent and tied together. There was a sadness there, later, after Mum and Dad had moved away. Our old neighbour, Mr Conlin, wandered down there one day when nobody was around and fell in and drowned. The Front Paddock was our cricket ground and football field. Dad would occasionally have a kick, but with his left foot because his rheumatics were too bad in his right leg. At other times, Noel and I would, separately, run round and round the paddock, training for football or maybe Olympic glory one day. How we drove ourselves! And how we dreamed!

* * *

Church was at half past two on Sunday afternoons. During the war, when clergy were scarce, lay readers like Mr Calderwood-Brown would often take the service. He drove down from Bunyip in his gig. To get to church, we'd walk through Phillips' up the hill from our place, across Barkers Road, and plunge down through the bush to come out behind the church. The same people were always there – Mrs Connelly and family, Mr and Mrs Parish and Bill, Mr and Mrs Pratt and family, Mrs Sippo (we'd sit with her), the Moores, the Basseds (sometimes we'd get a ride home with them), and a handful of others. Mr Pratt took up the collection during the last verse of the final hymn, agonisingly slowly, but always finishing in time. There were some beautiful words in the Prayer Book, like 'inheritance.' I waited for it with drawn breath and dried mouth. *'O Lord, save thy people: And bless thine inheritance.'* Overall, there was an aura of there being more to know than I already knew. I was quite content to wait patiently to enter into the fullness of knowledge in years to come. At Christmas, the men would sing an anthem. That was amazing! The most dramatic scene I have ever encountered occurred in church on an ordinary Sunday afternoon. The minister (Mr McSpedden, I think, from Drouin) was speaking in his sermon how all earthly things pass away. The great empires of the past have crumbled. Why, even the great British Empire will one day be no more. At that, Mrs Parish stopped him. She stood up at her organ stool and bellowed, "Never! Never! Never!" and sat down again. I was confirmed, along with Noel and some other children when I was fourteen. After the service, Bishop Blackwood gathered us into the vestry, gave us a lecture on the evils of alcohol, and got us all to sign the pledge. Even I could see the manipulation he was applying, but only one of us had the gumption to stand up to him, and that was Noel. To his everlasting credit and to my huge admiration, he said no.

* * *

Mum did the cooking, although Tessy and Angela helped at times. The only work bench was a rectangular table cut in half, placed against the kitchen wall. There was a small sink with a cold water tap over it. In the mornings we'd rush our breakfast to get off to school. For those going to High School, the bus left from the street at half past seven, so that meant leaving home by ten past. Porridge in the winter. An egg every morning. Mum would pack our lunches. For tea, there was often soup, and always meat and vegetables, and a pudding. There was a lot of talking, everybody joining in. In the middle of the meal, we would hear footsteps outside, there'd be a knock, the door would open, and Eily Conlin would come in. She would be on her way home from work, dressed in overalls. Eily worked packing apples for Parishes or doing seasonal work on the farms, with the hay or potatoes or asparagus. Later she worked at Miller's Rope Factory in Warragul. She'd lean against the door and watch us eat. Never would sit down. She'd join in the talk, that's all. Tessy was her favourite. Eily played basketball (now called netball) for Garfield and was very good. She had a soldier boyfriend at one time, which was extraordinary to a small boy like me, and she did marry later on – to someone else – and went to live in Warragul. I was at her funeral sixty years later. There was hardly anyone there.

On weekends, with Dad home, meal-times were sometimes very funny. We'd laugh at the foibles of some of the odd people round about, like Roger Hart, who took a cow to the Dandenong market. After he returned somebody asked him how he'd got on. *"They offered me a pound,"* he replied, *"but I told them I wouldn't take a penny less than seventeen and six."* Or there was the boy out on the Swamp who polished the furniture with butter. *"Aw, don't it shine!"* he said. Dad would tell us stories about the old days, like the one about the new chum ploughing. He was told to fix his eye on something ahead of him and go straight for it. When the boss came back, he found the furrows all over the place. *"But I did what you told me,"* the man exclaimed. *"I kept my eye on that old cow over on the hill."* Another one was about the prank of taking the horse out of the shafts, and putting him back in with a barbed wire fence between it and the gig. Or he'd tell us stories of Jonas Jackson, the clothesline robber in early Ballarat, or sing the song about Jack O'Rook (O'Rourke?) getting stuck in his chimney trying to get into his own house. One of the favourites was 'A Preacher went out Hunting.'

> *A preacher went out hunting;*
> *'Twas on a Sunday morn.*
> *And though it was against his religion,*
> *He took his gun along.*
> *Shot himself some very fine quail,*
> *And one little measly hare;*
> *And on his way returning,*
> *He met a great big grizzly bear.*

The preacher loses his gun and finds himself up a tree with the bear beneath. The preacher has this last resort.

> *O Lord, you delivered Daniel from the lion's den,*
> *And Jonah from the belly of the whale,*
> *And the Hebrew children from the fiery furnace,*
> *The good books do declare.*
> *Now Lord, indeed, if you can't help me,*
> *Then for goodness sake don't help that bear!*

But the absolute best, which we'd ask for again and again, was this (told with expression):

The two old farmers met each week as one was going to market and the other coming home. They were both men of very few words. Each week, they'd greet each other as they passed.

"Mornin' Si." "Mornin' Jos."

One day, however, it was different. Jos pulled on the reins and came to a stop. Likewise Si.

"Mornin' Si." "Mornin' Jos."

"What did you give your horse when it had the botts?"

"Turpentine."

"Mornin' Si." "Mornin' Jos."

The next week, Jos pulled up again.

"Mornin' Si." "Mornin' Jos."

Jos (rising voice) "What did you say you gave your horse when it had the botts?"

"Turpentine."

"Killed mine."

"Mine too."

"Mornin' Si." "Mornin' Jos."

* * *

Tessy was six years ahead of me, so I never went to school with her. My first year at Garfield State School was her first year at Warragul High School. My first year at Warragul High School was her first year at University. At Garfield, Mr Chappell arrived as Head Teacher, and lived in the house alongside the school. We got to know the Chappells well. The daughter, Norma, was Angela's friend. They sometimes came to our place. Mr Chappell was known as a left-winger. One time we were playing a game in the big drawing room. Tessy, who was blindfolded, would pull a name out of the hat and give that person a subject to speak on. It was Mrs Chappell's turn and Tessy gave her the subject, 'Joseph Stalin'. She began, *"Dear Mr Stalin, my husband is very fond of you."* We nearly killed ourselves trying not to laugh. We talked about it for years. Mr Chappell (Charlie) went out of his way to befriend Noel and me. Several times he took us down to Point Lonsdale when his family went for their summer holidays. Mr Chappell was captain of the Garfield cricket team, where Noel (and later I) played. Dad was sometimes furious with him because he batted too slowly or didn't give Noel a bowl.

We four Connelly children were generally acknowledged to be 'smart,' as the word was in those days, but Tessy was the smartest. She could do anything. Angela was good at sport, and both she and Tessy were excellent drawers and painters. Angela was outstanding. Noel was more practical, and also good at drawing. He always drew horses. I was sometimes paraded for my knowledge. Once, to my embarrassment, I was made by Mum to recite a poem in Mr Simcocks' shop, and he gave me a double-headed ice cream for doing it. I was very interested in horse-racing. Each Saturday I would study the paper and pick the winners. I did so well that Mum one day asked me which horse running that day was the most sure to win. I picked Dornford in the last race. She got Mr Conlin to put two shillings on it down at the pub, and he came home that night with seven and six for her. There was no second time! I used to do make-believe calls of the races. In one of the concerts in the Hall one year, just before the Melbourne Cup, I did a phantom call of the Cup, without notes. I was probably eight at the time. My interest in racing was stimulated by the fact that our 'cousin' Daphne, Aunty Vivien's daughter, and slightly younger than I, used to ride track work at Caulfield. They lived near the course, and before school she'd go down and ride with the likes of Jack Purtell and Scobie Breasley. I'd curl up in jealous agony when she told me about it. Dad would listen to the races on Saturday afternoons, then the boxing at night. The radio had a wet battery and a dry battery. The wet battery had to be re-charged at the garage every now and then, which was a great trouble because it had to be carried more than half a mile each way and was very heavy. When the charge ran out, the sound would fade away altogether. If there was something important or exciting on, we'd switch the radio off for half an hour and it would develop enough charge for us to listen for another ten minutes or so. Then the process would be repeated.

We all went to Garfield State School. To help the war effort part of the grass area where we kicked the football was turned into vegetable gardens. On Friday afternoons we stitched camouflage nets. Each week, those who could brought sixpence for a stamp to go into their war savings certificate. Thirty-two stamps (sixteen shillings) filled one certificate. Certificates could be redeemed for one pound five years later, though many didn't do so because of their patriotic feelings – or because they'd lost them! By the end of the war, children at the school had raised £111 through war savings certificates. One day a fighter plane flew so low over our heads it was gone almost before we knew it was there. Around us the road signs were taken down 'for the duration' and no lights could be shown at night. The cars and trucks had gas producers built on to the running boards, burning coke to power the vehicle. We had ration books for meat, sugar, tea, clothing, and petrol, though the petrol rationing didn't bother us as we had no car. There was no tea allowance until children were nine years old. There was great rejoicing in the family when each child reached that age. One day, a classmate of mine, Brian Leask, was away from school, and we heard that his brother had been killed when a Japanese submarine sank a hospital ship in Sydney Harbour. Men from around town would shock us by suddenly appearing in uniform. In 1941, Dad tried to join up, but was rejected as 'medically unfit.' He was forty-nine. In 1944, I started at Warragul High School. We had left our State School days behind us.

Garfield State School, number 2724. All four Connelly children attended school here, and two returned as teachers for short periods

Grade 1, Garfield State School, 1938. Yours truly in front

CHAPTER 10

One of the most significant people in our family history is our Aunty Vivien. Although not an actual family member, she has linked our family together across the generations in both England and Australia. Some of us have kept up with Vivien's family more than we have with our own. Vivien was originally Vivien Kendall. The Kendalls of Pelyn are an ancient and important family in English social and political history. Pelyn is a seventeenth-century estate at Lostwithiel in Cornwall. Daphne du Maurier has woven Pelyn and the Kendall family into her classic novel, 'My Cousin Rachel'. As a young woman, Vivien came to Caltofts to learn weaving from my grandmother, Margot Hazard. She stayed for a lengthy period, virtually as a member of the family. *"Life there was perfect, gracious and charming,"* she once wrote. She introduced her sister, Jill, to my mother, and it was as a result of this they travelled together to Australia. Affairs at Pelyn had turned very sour for Vivien and her mother, and they decided to also come out to Melbourne. Vivien, who had a propensity to fall in love, met Eric Plowright on board the 'Moldavia' on the way to Australia. He was one of the crew, and he was really two people in one – both charming and utterly unreliable, a drinker and gambler. Vivien suffered grievously at his hands. My mother was one of her few comforts, Aunty Janet being another. The two sisters, Vivien and Jill, were not close, and Jill returned to England, where she married, but sadly died in a riding accident during the Second World War. I've told how Mum stayed with Vivien at the time of my birth. Vivien would visit when she could at our various homes. I remember her often coming on the train from town, spending the day with us at Garfield, and returning that evening with some of Mum's lovely white bread. We looked forward hugely to her visits. Her daughter Daphne sometimes came to stay with us. We would sometimes visit Aunty Vivien when she was living at Caulfield. Mrs Kendall returned to England after some time, and took Daphne with her, ostensibly to 'finish her education'. Mrs Kendall died at Guernsey in the Channel Islands. For the last years of her life, Vivien lived in Williamstown. Her name at that time was 'Mrs Thomas'. There must have been a Mr Thomas at one time, but I can't remember him.

Vivien had two children. The older, Gerry, known locally as Ken, lives at Mansfield in rural Victoria, where he had a sports shop for many years. He married and had a family, though now is in a nursing home. Daphne, with her love of horses, has already been mentioned. She lived for more than fifty years in England. Daphne married Claude Banks, a farmer, from Kimbolton; they raised their three children there. In January 1996, Daphne had an extraordinary brush with death. After 'dying 'at home and being pronounced dead, she was lying in a mortuary when an assistant noticed minute signs of life. She was fully resuscitated and soon resumed her normal life. The news of this occurrence was flashed around the world's press, usually under the banner, *'The woman who came back from the dead'*. Daphne moved into a nursing home in nearby St Neots in 2015 and died there soon afterwards. Claude is well-known locally for his recent book of reminiscences, 'Once a Man – Twice a Boy'.

CHAPTER 11

The main street in Garfield has hardly changed in seventy years. Dr Paterson's home and surgery was in a grand, two-story house a little apart from the shops, as seemed appropriate. His sons, Ian and Peter, came to my seventh birthday party, when we all dressed in cowboy or redskin outfits. Dr Martin took over from Dr Paterson in 1941 or 1942. The Post Office was at the top end of town. In my early days, it was kept by the fearsome Mrs Drayson. Mail was kept in little pigeon-holes, and we'd ask for it at the counter. Every Thursday there was a tiny package of yeast for Mum to bake bread with. On the wall was a poster about putting the correct stamps on letters. *"Oh dear, fourpence tax. How annoying!"* a frowning lady was saying, who'd forgotten to put the twopenny stamp on her letter. Behind the partition we could hear the girl on the switchboard putting callers through on the manual exchange. Next door was the police station (it used to be alongside the school). Next came Jimmy Dean's garage, then Wall's baker's shop - white bread always, smelling delicious, and wrapped in tissue paper, half a loaf or a large loaf. Mostly, Mum baked our own, of course. Then, across the side road leading down to the football ground, there was Eric Edis's blacksmith shop. After school we'd gather at the entrance to watch him with his leather apron shoeing mighty, stamping horses, swearing away at them. He'd pump the bellows and the coals would glow. He'd take a horseshoe out of the coals and bash it into shape with his hammer. He'd plunge it into the cold water with a great fizz of steam. The picture theatre was alongside. Every Saturday night the pictures were on, and everybody seemed to go, always sitting in the same seats. Sometimes Noel and I went without any money. Noel was adept at attaching himself to a large family party and walking in undetected. Les Haigh had a butcher's shop next door to the theatre. Later, Jimmy Fawkner, our football captain, took it over. Then came Jack Phillips' soft goods shop, where I worked on Christmas Eve when I was old enough, to help with the rush. The Phillips were friends of ours. They lived next to us, about half a kilometre away. A private house was alongside Mr Phillips' store, where the Jonas family lived. Then Barnes' sweets shop, followed by Mr Lombardo's barber's shop. You walked down the passage past where he was cutting hair to the billiard saloon, a place of dark mysteries. Then came Mr Simcocks' shop, which was the hub of the town. He sold newspapers, ice cream, and tobacco amongst other things. Sometimes I would buy Dad's tobacco for him. Mr Simmy would pull it out surreptitiously from under the counter. This was during the war and it was in short supply. Two ounces of Havelock ready-rubbed and a packet of Tally-ho cigarette papers was the usual order.

There were two grocer's shops – Nutting's and Edney's, although we drove the horse and cart to Bunyip, five kilometres away, every second Saturday to get feed for the cows and the chooks. Nutting's sold Bushells tea and Edney's sold Robur. We dealt with Nutting's, because we knew them well. Beth Nutting was a friend of Tessy's and Robert Nutting came to live with us for six months as a war evacuee from Melbourne when the Nuttings moved there. They bought a historic home in Black Rock – Black Rock House – and we children stayed there

Main Street, Garfield. It was here we would catch the school bus to Warragul High School

sometimes. When Noel and I went, Mr Nutting would have jobs ready for us, like hacking though the base of a huge Moreton Bay fig so he could gain a back access to his garage. He was a hard man. The two grocer's shops were separated by the Bank – the English, Scottish and Australian, ESA. Here I proudly opened my first account with five shillings. Where that came from I can't imagine. We schoolchildren would talk about how the manager slept with a loaded revolver under his pillow. Then came a vacant block, with Keith Sarah, the chemist, next, and a second butcher's shop, Con Breman's, who played cricket with us. Then another sweets shop run by Mr and Mrs Whelan. The hotel followed, towards the lower end of the street. It was to me a place of mystery and danger. Strange things were said to occur there, and there was the bitter smell of beer as we walked past. None of us ever went to the pub, except Noel, after he started to play football. There was no alcohol at home. Almost at the end of the street was Mr Interlighi, who was the bootmaker. He was regarded with some suspicion during the war years. The Italian prisoners-of-war who worked on the asparagus farm on the Swamp used to congregate at his shop. Last of all, near the corner with the 13-Mile Road, was Ham's garage, which became Brenchleys' about the time the war ended.

On the other side of the road was the railway station. In wartime, it was 'browned-out' like all the houses, and there were posters warning against careless talk. *'The Walls Have Ears,'* one proclaimed. Another asked, *'Is Your Journey Really Necessary?'* If we were going to Melbourne to stay with Aunty Vivien in Caulfield or Aunty Janet in St Albans or to go to the football, we'd catch the ten to seven train. In winter, it would still be dark, and the lights of the approaching train and the deep growl of the engine would excite our imaginations beyond words. Across the railway line was Parish's packing shed. After school, we'd congregate at the large open side door and watch the apples tumbling into the bins from the conveyor belt and the packers as they grasped each apple, wrapped it in tissue with a flick of the wrist, and set it in its patterned place in the wooden case. We'd stand there until Mr Parish threw us some apples, and we'd go away. Between the packing shed and the school was the Hall. There used to be concerts every now and then, with the Connelly family appearing in plays, sometimes written by my mother. The dances were held here on Saturday nights, sometimes with a band and sometimes just Mrs Bassed on the piano. A church group of mysterious origin met here on Sundays. Their sign at the front read, *'The Gospel will be preached here, if the Lord wills, on Sunday next at 2.00 pm'*. Our church was further along the road, past the school.

CHAPTER 12

The State School played a big part in our lives. To get to school, we turned off our track, struck through the bush for half a kilometre, got on to the main road, down the hill, then ducked in behind the Methodist Church to the back of the schoolground. There was a rough cricket pitch there, but I don't remember much cricket being played. More I remember the clod fights we had in the back corner of the school grounds, where the clay soil provided magnificent ammunition. There were some really big kids at school – the ones who went on to Grade 8. They would have been fourteen, turning fifteen. Those of us going to High School left after Grade 6. The biggest boys belonged to a terrifying gang that met in the ti-tree behind the main street. Terrible tales were told of how they treated their enemies, all of them, I now realise, hugely exaggerated. I lived in fear of them, but somehow escaped their attention. There were three rooms in the school. The Little Room had Grades 1 and 2, the Middle Room Grades 3 and 4, and the Big Room all the others. In the Little Room there was a poster above the door about cleaning one's teeth regularly. A smiling lady squeezing toothpaste on to a toothbrush recommended regular toothcleaning. *'Half an inch on a dry brush is sufficient'*, the caption read. Miss Maynard was one of my first teachers. There was another teacher called Mrs Cooper. She sometimes brought her small son, too young to be enrolled, with her. We used to laugh at him and called him 'Ash-lar.' His real name was Ashley and he grew up to be a famous tennis player. In Grade 1 one day we were writing fractions as words. Miss Maynard told us she was going to come along and give each of us a ruler on the hand if we hadn't put the hyphen between the words, like 'one-half.' She had been warning us about it. She started at the front of the row. I hadn't been putting in the hyphen, and I started to put them in as fast as I could go. By the time she got to me I was crying. I was only five. It was too much for me to cope with. I'll never forget how I felt as she came closer and closer, with me going to pieces and trying to find all the places where I hadn't put in the hyphen.

I remember a spelling test when I was in Grade 2. There were eighty words and I got seventy-nine right, but I was upset because there was a new girl in the class – Jocelyn Mauger – and she got eighty! The school dentist would come from time to time and we would be called out in pairs to his van. He came one day to call the next two on the list - me and Ronnie Cox. *'Jim Tim Connelly and Connie Rox'* he said. Everyone roared laughing. In between his visits, if we needed a dentist, we went to the man who came to the Supper Room at the back of the Hall on Saturday mornings and pulled out our teeth. I don't remember him ever doing anything other than that. In the Big Room, if I finished my work early, I would try to do the work Mr Chappell was giving the bigger kids. He gave me the strap once, most unfairly. I was innocent, but I was in bad company! Later on I was the sole witness to a sensation. I was in Grade 6, sitting by myself in the back seat, and could see out the side window because the floor was tiered. The night before there had been some trouble down near the rubbish tip, and four young fellows had been arrested by Mr Pringle, (or was it Mr O'Halloran then?) That was a thrilling event and the whole school was talking about it. From my desk I could see the back yard of the police station and the lock-up. I saw these four being let out for a break. They were walking freely around the yard. Then, to my astonishment, I watched as they made a concerted rush for the fence, leapt over it, and ran off into the bush. There was some shouting from Mr Pringle. He chased the men into the bush, but soon returned alone, although we heard they were caught some time later. I was able to give a point-by-point account to all the others when we got out for lunch.

The entrance exam for Warragul High School was at the school in Bunyip. That meant riding my bike there, together with Mavis Johnson, the only other one from Garfield going on to High School that year. As a young boy, and with the other two and then three going off to Warragul on the bus each day, I came to imagine that there was really no such place as Warragul High School. It was an invention, a creature of imagination. Or rather, it was a place of eternal happiness, a heaven, not one to be waited and longed for as the minister spoke about at church, but now here, its existence conspiratorially kept from me by everybody else. The day came when the reality was revealed to me. I trod the earth of this fabled place. The House system was very strong. Tessy had been in Lyall House. Angela and Noel were in Haines. When I arrived as a new boy, I was drafted into Swinburne! I was deeply distressed. Mum wrote a note the next day and I was re-drafted into Lyall. The sun shone once more. There was a technical wing to the school, but I was not destined for that. The entrance exam had pointed me to the regular, more academic stream, it seems. There was still a large drop-out rate. 132 of us started in Form 1 in 1944; there were fifteen in Form 6 in my final year, 1949. School enrolment constantly overflowed the buildings. One of my matriculation classes was in the staff room, another on the front veranda, another in the Principal's office. I don't think we were taught well. Not in a general educational sense. I can't remember a single time when a member of the staff gave me particular encouragement or identified any special abilities. There were few light-bulb moments. One was in Form 3 Science, when Mr Greenwell used the word, 'ecology' and explained it. None of us had heard the word before. For the first time, I glimpsed how all things might hang together. I was quite content with school life especially in the higher forms. In the lower school, I was mad for football and cricket. I thought of little else, and spent every recess and lunch-time on the school oval. One of my proudest moments was when I was made Captain of the 1st X1 in my final year (as Noel had been before me).

CHAPTER 13

Now to us four children. If I go into more detail here, it's because I have in mind the following generations, who may be curious about their more immediate family.

Tessy (Teresa Ann) was born in 1927. She was only sixteen when she started university, and had completed her B.Sc. at nineteen. She had been Dux of Warragul High School and Captain of the school. At university, she majored in Bio-Chemistry, and found her first job at the Blood Bank in the City. It wasn't long, however, before she came back to West Gippsland as the Bio-Chemist in charge of the laboratory at the Drouin Butter Factory. She was there for several years, continuing after her marriage to Keith Towt, which was at our church in Garfield. Keith came from a pioneering timber and orcharding family from Garfield North. He played cricket for Garfield as a fast bowler and rode a motor-bike dangerously fast. He and Tessy built a small home at Garfield North, but the marriage lasted only a couple of years. It was a serious mis-match. They had nothing in common. Keith had no feeling for the higher or broader things of life, whereas Tessy was educated; she painted, was a lover of modern art, a conservationist and bush-walker, and had advanced views on social issues.

Tessy was very kind by nature. Angela remembers that when, as children, the two of them had chores to do, Tessy would finish her own, then help Angela with hers. When I was small and felt neglected, it was Tessy who was alert to this and came to my rescue. For instance, one day, at a time when I was the only one not at High School, Tessy arranged with me that I would go and hide in the bush as the other three walked home from the bus. She would find a pretext to dawdle behind the other two, then I would come out from the bush and join her. I can remember the excitement as I waited in the bush and the warmth I felt as we walked home together. Tessy once made me a marvellous picture-story book about cowboys and Indians, written and illustrated by herself, and sewn skilfully into booklet form. She was the thoughtful one; she could cope with anything. When she received a letter, she would read it, screw it up, and throw it away. She could remember everything in it. As an adult, she would impulsively give her personal possessions away to someone who lacked them. When my mother-in-law mentioned she didn't have a watch, Tessy took hers off her wrist and gave it to her.

Tessy's son, Stephen, was born some time after the split with Keith, and, needing to earn an income, Tessy returned to work. She was at the Veterinary Research Institute in Parkville for quite a long time. She tried teaching, first at Moe High School for a short time, then at St Margaret's School in Berwick, and later at Mentone Girls Grammar School. But she disliked teaching. At Moe, the students were impossible. She found the atmosphere at St Margaret's hard to bear, though the girls she found likeable, but precious. She was not the sort to bend herself to fit in. Rather, she left. My mother looked after Stephen quite a lot during this time. Then came Tessy's marriage to Jim Webster, a technician in the Air Force. She and Stephen went with him to Ipswich in Queensland where he was based for some years, then, after Jim came back to Laverton Air Base near Melbourne, they lived in Bundoora, a Melbourne suburb. Stephen did very well at school in Queensland and in Melbourne. Soon after he had begun at Melbourne University, Tessy became ill. The diagnosis was the worst possible – terminal lung cancer. Probably it was linked to the breast cancer she had gone through and seemed to have beaten while in Queensland. She spent most of the months of her illness with Angela and Ewen on their farm at Vervale, near Garfield, with Stephen and Jim visiting constantly. Thanks to Angela's care, Tessy was able to stay there until almost the end. She died in Bunyip Hospital, and the funeral service was in our old church at Garfield. Tessy is buried in the Bunyip Cemetery. It was July, 1974; Tessy was forty-seven.

Stephen was twenty when his mother died. He went on to complete an Arts degree at Melbourne University, then a B.Phil. at Oxford and a B.Ed. While there he married Phillippa Twomey, a fellow-student from Melbourne days. Stephen taught for some years in England and later in Melbourne, after their return home. He then studied Librarianship and made his career in that field, becoming successively Law Librarian at Melbourne University, then Librarian at the United Faculty of Theology, a position he has held for the past fourteen years. Stephen has taken the name of 'Connelly'. Phillippa has had a career in Social Work, then in tertiary administration, being at one time Dean of Students at Ormond College, and later Principal of Medley Hall, a residential college of Melbourne University, her current position. There are four children – Alexander, Rosamund, Marina and Astrid. Alex lives and works in Melbourne;

Rosamund studied Dramatic Art in England, later married, and now lives in London with her husband, Jeremy, and their two children, Thomasina and Mary; Marina obtained an Open Scholarship to Harvard and is currently completing a PhD there; Astrid is finishing her degree in Music at the Melbourne Conservatorium. Astrid sings beautifully. Alex, Marina, and Astrid are visually-impaired as a result of their albinism.

* * *

Angela (Angela Frances) was born in 1928, a year and six weeks after Tessy. She remembers starting school at North Creswick. She also vividly remembers being trapped in the drum at Pearcedale, as previously reported. She finished school at Garfield and went on to Warragul High School. Angela made friends easily and was a good storyteller. At home we would be spellbound by the stories of her doings, and, later, when she had left home, by her marvellous letters. One day she brought home a dog from Warragul High. She had found it shivering in the frost near the school bus stop and rescued it. She called it 'Gypsy.' It was the first dog I ever knew. Soon we acquired another — a big mutt called 'Bulldozer.' (They had a sad end, however. Two or three years later, they attacked the chooks and killed many of them. Once a killer, always a killer, we children were told, so early one dreadful Saturday morning, Bill Parish came round with his gun and took the two dogs off into the bush. I lay cowering under the bedclothes in the sleep-out waiting for the inevitable gun-shots.) Angela was a good hockey player and basket-baller, and a good actor. At High School, she and one or two others would put on humorous items at lunch-time to raise money for charity. We were all involved in acting, actually. We often played charades at home. Real charades, old-fashioned charades.

Angela was also Captain of School at Warragul High in her final year, then spent a year teaching at first Bunyip State School, then at Garfield. She went on to teacher training in Melbourne, living in the Teachers College in Carlton. As part of her training, she took up an extension to do part of an Arts degree at Melbourne University. Amazing tales of College life were retailed to us back at home by letter or in person. One summer holiday, she organised forty girls to go to Snug in Tasmania to pick berries. That was Angela! Her first appointment was to Murtoa Higher Elementary school. More exciting tales arrived home. By this time, Angela and Ewen - Ewen Costain, a farmer and farmer's son from Vervale, near Garfield - had become what we'd call an item these days. So Angela's teaching career was curtailed as she and Ewen were married, again in the Garfield church. They started life in a caravan alongside Ewen's parents' farm-house, but moved into the house itself before long. Ewen and his brother, Ian, who also lived on the property, worked their dairy-farm in partnership. After having her family, Angela resumed her career, teaching French and remedial subjects in local high schools. Both she and Ewen were very involved in golf throughout the district. Angela was a superb artist in water colours and oils. She won many awards, and her paintings hang in dozens of homes throughout Gippsland. Angela and Ewen were on the farm for over fifty years, until Ewen's death in 2006. Soon afterwards, the farm was sold, and Angela moved into a unit in Garfield for five or six years before moving to residential accommodation, 'Amberlea' in nearby Drouin. Angela in later years had been in continual poor health, and needed the security of greater care.

There are three children, Rodney, Meredith, and Lyndel. All three went to Iona State School, then Drouin High School, before going off to Haileybury in the case of Rodney and Firbank for Meredith and Lyndel. Rodney trained as a metallurgist and had a long and successful career in that field, principally at Ballarat. Rodney is now retired and lives in Ballarat. He was married to Kathy Neeson, a teacher, and there are three children - Matthew, Scott and Simon. Each one completed their schooling at St Pius College in Sydney and went on to graduate from Sydney University, Matthew in Engineering, Scott in Accountancy, and Simon in Economics/Marketing. Matthew is now a General Manager with SBS television; Scott is an owner partner in a firm of Chartered Accountants; and Simon is Marketing Manager with an Education Service. All live in Sydney and have many interests, ranging from mountain biking, music, disc-jockeying, cricket and cycling to salsa dancing and event organising. Scott is married to Emma; they have three children – Oliver, Thomas and Benjamin. Meredith did an Arts degree and, after a stint as a teacher, became a highly-acknowledged writer for children. Her partner is Paul Collins, a writer and publisher of Young Adult literature. They live in Clifton Hill in Melbourne. Lyndel trained as a dietician and has been very successful. She has written and spoken widely in that field. She has lived in Britain for over twenty years, conducting an extensive private practice, and was at one time spokesperson for the British Dietetic Association. Lyndel is married to Steve

Denny, now retired from his work as Chief Executive of a wholesale Cash and Carry business, and rejoices in her step-granddaughter, Iris.

* * *

Noel (William Noel) was born in 1930. He started school at Pearcedale, but was there for a very short time before we moved to Garfield. Then like Tessy and Angela before him, he went through Garfield State School and on to Warragul High School. But there was a variation to the established pattern, because after two years Noel switched to Caulfield Technical School, where he was destined for the carpentry trade. That meant a long train trip each morning and afternoon. Sometimes he came home with his schoolbag filled with briquettes. His train had stopped alongside one of the huge trains that carried briquettes from Yallourn to Melbourne. Enough said! He also brought home stories of happenings at school of tough students and tough teachers. He brought joy to me because he also brought home the craze of rolling up the trade aprons the boys used at Tech and using them as footballs. I played many games of league football by myself in the yard at home using these footballs and starring for Essendon in every match I played. Noel resumed at Warragul High after two years and remained there until Form 6, when he left to begin his career as a surveyor with the firm of Ross and Worth in Warragul.

Noel was a good all-round sportsman – a middle-distance runner, cricketer and footballer. At cricket he could open the bowling or bowl leg spinners. He was more a bowler than a batsman, though he made a century for Garfield once, I remember. At football, he played for Garfield for some years, and also for Newborough and Nilma at different times. Although he was not really tall (just under six feet), he played as a ruckman and won a fine reputation as one of the best tap ruckmen in the game. Dad was at every home game to see him – football and cricket, both - and at the away games also, if he could get a ride. At home later, each game would be dissected and if Noel hadn't been best on the ground, Dad could explain it through the foul machinations of the opposing team, or even our own! Later in his life, Noel became a good golfer, but he turned to bowls and was quite a champion at his club, Yallourn, and further afield. Through his sport, Noel made a lot of friends. Like Angela, he mixes easily and people appreciate his sense of humour. Of all four of us, Noel has perhaps been the one to move most easily and naturally in the local scene.

At the age of twenty-one, Noel went to Papua New Guinea as a surveyor with an oil search company. This involved him in difficult and often dangerous survey work in the swampy south of the country, living rough, in charge of native assistants, and called on to make challenging decisions. After three and a half years he returned, completed his studies to gain his Qualified Surveyor's licence in 1961 and married a local girl, Joyce Harker. The Harkers were a long-established local farming family. Joyce was well-known to all of us. She and her brother, Francis, were members of the Presbyterian Church, and so friends of Ewen and Ian Costain. The wedding was in the Presbyterian Church in Bunyip, and it must have been in the football season because Noel had some sort of football injury and found trouble in kneeling where he was supposed to in the service. Noel and Joyce lived in Newborough and then Warragul for a time before moving to Yallourn – the model town of the 1920s built for State Electricity Commission workers, and later demolished to make way for further mining. Noel spent almost all his working life with the SEC – thirty years in all – many of them as Principal Surveyor of the Latrobe Valley Region. After his retirement he did a good deal of surveying work privately.

When the township of Yallourn was being dismantled, Noel and Joyce bought two of the houses and had them transported to their block of land at Westbury on the outskirts of Moe. They were put together to form one large home. Noel had fifty acres there, and ran beef cattle in conjunction with his work with the SEC and then after his retirement. He treated his stock with loving care and often topped the market with his fat cattle. Joyce played bowls and did voluntary work at her local opportunity shop. She went to a painting group and did some nice pieces. And she was a wonderful seamstress. Joyce and Noel adopted two children – Jenny and Alan. Jenny married Robert Hirsch, who was a fitter and turner by trade. They lived in Western Australia for some years. On their return they came back to Moe, not far from Joyce and Noel. There are three children – Damien, Jessica, and Holly. Jessica is married to Shane Pope. They live in Warragul, and there are two children, Jasmine and Lucas, great-grandchildren for Noel. Alan followed Jenny and Rob to Western Australia, but developed a serious mental illness while there, and since has been unable to work. For many years he has lived in his own unit alongside Noel. Sadly, Joyce died in 2003. In 2014, Noel bought another place, in Newborough, close by, and fitted out a living space for Alan at the rear of the house. Noel was fortunate to find a good friend and bowls companion, in another Joyce – Joyce Wardley – but, sad to record, she also died, in 2012. Noel keeps good health and is very active in everyday affairs.

*   *   *

I'm James Timothy, born in July, 1933. One of my earliest memories is of a row between my parents. I remember my mother sitting on the edge of her bed pulling her stockings on, and crying. She was trying to get to church. I remember the outbreak of war, Mum being very upset and showing me pictures in the paper of German war-planes. There were many happy times. Waking up on Christmas morning was exciting beyond words, feeling the stocking filled with presents at the bottom of the bed. Once, Mum got a friend, Mrs Mason, to make me a shirt-and-pants set, with a penny in every pocket. A little later, there were endless hours of playing cricket with Noel in the front paddock, or football in season. But I was often alone because of the others being at school in Warragul. I used to dream of life's possibilities. I'd lie on my back in the paddock, watching the clouds, and trying to work out the big questions of life, though I always kept my speculations to myself.

During my High School days, Bill Parish resurrected the Scout Troop, with Fred Cox the Assistant Scoutmaster. That took all my Friday nights for some years, and there were camps in the holidays as well. Noel began to play first cricket and then football with Garfield and I followed suit two or three years later. Noel was more a bowler; I was more a batsman. Noel was a ruckman; I was a rover. These things took a large part of our time and our thinking. In my last year at High School, I won a Studentship to do an Arts degree and Dip. Ed. at Melbourne University, but I was still only sixteen and too young to be admitted to University. To fill in the year, I spent 1950 as a Student Teacher at Garfield State School. Mum and I were the only ones at home by then, with Dad also on the weekends. At the end of my first year at uni, I did my National Service – three months training at Puckapunyal, followed by two years of fortnightly parades and annual camps. I returned to take up a place in an Education Department hostel in Victoria Street, Carlton, where I remained, very happily, for the next three years. Together with two others from the hostel, I played football with the University Blacks.

My first appointment, in 1955, was to teach English and Social Studies at Wangaratta Technical School. My teaching duties were not onerous. I played cricket and football with the Wangaratta Rovers. For two years I lived at the Church of England hostel for secondary school boys in Cathedral Close, as a Housemaster. The Church was a big part of my life. I was President of the Young Anglican Fellowship. Anne Walker was the secretary. Custom decreed that the President should marry the Secretary and so it was - but not for a little while. I left Wangaratta at the end of 1957 to become an Assistant Master at Cranbrook School, Sydney. In May of the following year, Anne and I were married in Wangaratta Cathedral. Anne was a colourist in the laboratory at Wangaratta Woollen Mills. She had migrated with her family – father, mother, sister and brother - from England in 1954.

Anne and I were at Cranbrook for fourteen years. Cranbrook, of course, was established in the great house built by my great-grandfather, Robert Tooth. For two years, from 1962 to 1964, we were on exchange at Oundle School in Northamptonshire. Elizabeth and Catherine were born before we went to England, Christopher was born over there, and Richard while we were in Street House, one of the Boarding Houses, after our return to Cranbrook. In 1972, I moved to Canberra Grammar School, and managed to complete an M.Ed. while there. They were good years. We bought a block of bushland at Araluen, and spent as much time as we could camping there. After five years in Canberra, I was appointed as the founding Principal of the Christian Community College in Portland, Victoria. This was an inter-denominational co-educational secondary school, which grew out of an existing Loreto College. We had five extraordinarily hard years there, though the College did well, and has become, nearly forty years on, a flourishing establishment, now named Bayview College.

Towards the end of my last year at Portland, I was accepted as an ordinand by the Bishop of Gippsland, and was ordained Deacon early in 1982, then priested ten months later. The first year was spent at Trinity College in Melbourne. That was followed by a year as Associate Priest in Traralgon Parish, before we went to our first solo parish, Neerim South, a Co-operating Parish with the Uniting Church. In 1987, I was appointed to Maffra, where we spent ten very happy and fulfilling years. In 1991, we had ten months overseas, while a Locum looked after the parish. Anne took up a four-month Churchill Fellowship in ecclesiastical embroidery at Manchester Polytechnic, while I acted as Locum Vicar of Mellor Parish, Stockport. Later we had shorter locum placements in Scotland, London, and Northern Ireland. I retired from active ministry in 1997.

After her schooling in Canberra, Elizabeth studied Dental Therapy in Hobart. After her return to Canberra, she worked as a Dental Therapist until music took over, and she became a highly-successful teacher of piano. Elizabeth is married to Gordon Fyfe and has continued in Canberra, Gordon now retired after a career in the Public Service, and Elizabeth still at work. Elizabeth and Gordon have two children, Douglas and Karen. Douglas is working as a Pastor at a Chinese church in Sydney. He is married to Jayme Lo, and they have two boys, Elias and Callum. Karen, also a music teacher in Canberra, is married to Anthony da Silva. They live in Canberra with Anthony's two children, Kayla and Jack. Catherine went on from the College in Portland to do Social Work at Warrnambool. She married Greg Love, though the marriage did not last. Teresa was born in 1985. She was first married to Joe Brennan, and now to Troy Wright, and has three children, Austin, Marley, and Hamish. Teresa is a nurse. After some years as a Social Worker, Catherine also moved more and more into music. She is a Celtic harpist, retreat leader and spiritual director. Catherine lives in Upwey with her partner, Roger Mazzolini, a Cathodic Protection manager in the gas industry. Christopher also finished his schooling in Portland, then studied Analytical Chemistry at

RMIT. He began work with the Environment Protection Authority, but later did an MBA, and has moved into the managerial field, currently in Melbourne conducting his own IT management consultancy firm – Cache Group. He has been a senior officer in the Army Reserves for many years. Christopher was first married, briefly, to Allason Price and later to Andrea Eunson. They live in inner Melbourne, and have two children, Harrison and Charlotte. Richard was at the College in Portland, but finished school at Gippsland Grammar. For several years he worked on a peach orchard-cum-cattle station in Araluen. He moved then to work in Batemans Bay on the NSW coast, where he indulged in his loves of sailing and flying, but had to relinquish flying when he developed diabetes at the age of twenty-two. He then came to Melbourne and worked with the Department of Human Services while studying law. He is now in sole legal practice in Warragul, specialising in Family Law. In 2000, Richard married Annette Sanders, a paediatrician, now at the Latrobe Regional Hospital here in Gippsland. They live in our former place at Buln Buln East. There are three children, Lucy, Simon, and Thomas.

After my retirement in 1997, Anne and I moved to a house with twenty-acres at Buln Buln East, near Warragul, and lived there until 2011. We have both been heavily involved in the University of the Third Age. Anne has continued with her ecclesiastical embroidery. In 2003, I completed a PhD at Monash University, and in 2005, we did volunteer work for three months with the Church in Rwanda. Latterly, I have tried my hand at writing for children, and have published three books. In 2011, Richard and Annette bought our Buln Buln East property, and we moved into the township of Warragul.

CHAPTER 14

When I left for Melbourne in 1951, it meant that Mum and Dad were alone at home, though for another few years Dad was away during the week with the Forestry Commission. Mum busied herself in the church and town (and writing letters to each of us). There were also the chooks and the garden. By now she had a car – a little Ford, bought second-hand - which had a canvas hood that could be taken back. Dad never drove. Mum also had a dog for company, a blue roan Cocker Spaniel, named Nell. We children came home quite often, and Mum continued to sometimes take in boarders, like a young man from the Bank or a single woman schoolteacher. Angela and Ewen were fairly near, and Tessy, also, for some of this time. Things were better domestically. The house was now connected with the town's water supply, and a kerosene refrigerator had replaced the old cool cupboard and Coolgardie safe. About this time, too, the old front section of the house was entirely remodelled. There was a new kitchen and a concrete front veranda. After he retired, Dad was at something of a loss. He would sit on the raised roots of the large gum tree between the house and the front paddock, smoking and grumbling away to himself. Due no doubt to his smoking, his general health was deteriorating.

Within a year or two of Dad's retirement, Mum and Dad sold up the Garfield place and bought a small home in Patterson Street, Carrum, an outer Melbourne suburb. It was a good move. Mum quickly developed a new set of connections in the near neighbourhood. Her letters to me were full of witty comment on the goings-on in the street. Each of us children spent time there, and by now there were grandchildren to be taken as well. The beach was not far away, and Mum would go for walks there, bringing back seaweed to dig into the sandy soil, along with the household scraps, to enrich the garden. The railway station was not far away. Mum went to church at Chelsea. More witty comment about the aged priest who presided there! As for Dad, he had few of these interests, though he, too, maintained a lively watch on things around him. His bronchitis was getting worse, and he was spending more and more time in bed. His heart eventually gave out under the considerable strain it was under, and he died, at home, in July, 1961. He was sixty-nine.

Mum was now freer to go away. When we sailed to England in 1962, she followed a few months later on a twelve-passenger trading vessel. In England, Mum spent most of her time between us in Northamptonshire and her sister Rosalind's place in Worcestershire. She came with us on a four-week caravan trip around the south of England, and also had a couple of weeks on a tour of Wales, keeping a diary of each day's events. Mum never lost her ability to be enthusiastic and to be excited by new things. We all spent our Christmases with Rosalind. On one occasion, Anne and I took Mum back to Caltofts. It was more than forty years since she had seen it last. We were very worried that the visit would be a failure, and that it would have been better to leave Mum's memories as they were, especially as we knew the place was much changed. It was then being used as a preparatory school. However, the visit went wonderfully well. Mum went all over the house and grounds with great joy. None of the emotional sentimentality we had feared. Not long after, Mum had a heart attack, and spent four or five weeks in a rehabilitation centre near Northampton. She was never strong again after that, though she was able to come back to Australia by sea with us and resume her life in Carrum. Four years later, in September, 1968, after some weeks in hospital, she died at the age of sixty-seven. An obituary in the Bunyip and Garfield Express commented, 'She will be remembered for her capacity to befriend people and in particular those in need of help or reassurance.' She is buried in Cheltenham cemetery with my father.

POSTSCRIPT

Partly as a tribute to my mother and partly because they may explain something of how she saw her own life, I include one of her poems and one of her short stories. Readers are invited to make of them what they will.

Untitled

The trumpet blew, an angel called out "Next!"

A farmer's wife stepped forward, rather vexed.

She had excuses, yes, she had a lot to say –

She should have been in Paradise today,

Not called before a Court! What had she done,

Who always worked so hard, and had no fun?

She hadn't often shown a helping hand,

But she was busy – God would understand.

He knew – He must – how women worked all day,

How scraping saucepans wore their soul away.

Yes, she had nagged the children, nagged at Dad,

Thank Goodness life was over – she was glad.

"Next!" cried the angel, as he blew once more.

Another woman stood within the door.

She said, "I must not hope for Heaven twice,

For fifty years I've had my Paradise.

For every year was joy, and every hour,

And every child I toiled for, every flower -

I lived among great trees of rich delight

Oh God, have you heard crickets in the night?

Did not some thrush once crack your heart with pain?

Oh, may I not go home, and live again?"

"I had all that!" cried she who spoke before,

And weeping bitterly, passed through the door.

J.W. Connelly, Garfield

Pinelands

by J.W. Connelly, 'Winston,' Garfield

"Pinelands", the man at the cobbler's shop had said as he accepted the young man's suit-cases. "Oh, yes. It's about four miles out, I reckon. Go up the road out of town, turn to your left, and ask again. Oh yes, your cases'll be all right here till this evening. They won't be no trouble to me".

If he gave them a puzzled stare from under his shaggy eyebrows, they didn't notice it, as they swung happily away into the golden morning, devouring eagerly all the new sights and sounds of a brand-new country. Australia, after only three days of it, was still a huge adventure.

Michael was tall and fair, and almost 20; Peter was tall and dark, and had left his twentieth birthday behind him, in England. They were cousins, and had always done everything together – from teething to emigrating. They walked along together now, discussing their project of today, but in the intervals of many distractions. First there were children coming into the township to school. Australian children! Then there were the magpies – magpies everywhere! - and the entrancing burst of kookaburra laughter – and the scattered houses, and the trim, wire-fenced paddocks, and the stringy-stemmed wild-flowers. It was all so different.

Peter said: "Not having anyone to meet us most likely means that Aunt Julia did not get my letter".

And Michael said, "Do you think she'll mind our bursting in at 10 o'clock in the morning?"

But Peter pointed out that 10 o'clock in the morning was almost equivalent to midday on a sheep-station, that everyone, including Aunt Julia, would have been up since 5 a.m., if not before. And day or night, expected or unexpected, Aunt Julia would welcome them with open arms, the nephews she had never seen. It was just at this point that a pair of kookaburras burst into a wild fit of sardonic laughter just overhead, but Peter scoffed at the notion that <u>they</u> knew a thing or two about Aunt Julia's welcome!

"Why, I know Aunt Julia", he declared. "I've read all her letters for years. The old girl never misses her monthly epistle, and never has, for thirty years. And they're good! She's witty, and she's shrewd - as sharp as a needle, I'll bet, but good-hearted and she always sees the funny side. We're going to like our old auntie, Mike!"

"Our old auntie can't be much more than a mile away" hazarded Michael, "if that old fellow knows what a mile means. And by the way, did you hear that the old girl wasn't always on such good terms with the rest of us? Isn't it a fact there was a big family row in the medieval days, and all surrounding Aunt Julia?"

Peter knew all about it. Somehow his Australian aunt had always been a specially romantic figure to Peter. There had been a row, a very bad row, about Aunt Julia's romance. She was not very young when the Australians marched into her home town in 1916, and she had already fallen indiscreetly in love, and had been badly snubbed by her family. Then she fell indiscreetly in love once more, this time with an Australian soldier. Apparently, a mere Australian soldier, without so much as a stripe, with no background, no relations or recommendations whatever, and a perfectly dreadful mode of speech. There was consternation in the family circle, but Julia was no longer a child, by any means, and Julia accepted, and in the face of all opposition, <u>wore</u> a large, cheap ring - a vulgar ring! The soldier marched away, but the ring remained. After the war, Julia announced that she was going out to Australia to marry him – and that was the last that anyone had seen of her.

"I should think, said Peter, "they all felt rather ashamed of themselves after that. Apparently, not one of our esteemed aunts, uncles, or parents even went to see the steamer bear her off – or was it sailing-ships in those antique days?"

"And after all, what <u>was</u> it all about?" demanded Michael. "Her soldier turned out to be the owner of a sheep-station. He had pots of money and their kids were as clever as they were beautiful and good. I believe it's grandchildren now, isn't it?"

"Two", said Peter, absently. "Blue eyes and curly hair – paragons absolutely. Oh yes, I suppose in a way, Aunt Julia could afford to be generous when everything turned out so well for her, and so badly for us. I don't grudge her the little heaps of gold – nor her two cars, nor the new hot-water system she has been filling her last few letters with. I think she deserves them all. But to come down to hard tacks, Michael, do you realise we can't be far from our famous sheep-station? We've been walking off and on for an hour and a half. Now, what is the next turning going to bring to our view?"

"Well, if it brings a sheep-station to our view, I shall be surprised", said Michael sceptically. "By this time we should hear the sheep. Several thousand sheep must be capable of raising a terrific din".

"They don't cackle like hens", pointed out his cousin, "and they won't be grouped all together in a paddock beside the house. But all the same, next time we come to a house, we'll ask. We might be on the wrong road all the time".

The road which might be the wrong one began from the next turning to wind slowly up the hill. There was sparse cultivation in the paddocks on either side, and a few cows, but of sheep, neither sight nor sound.

"We shall have to ask", decided Michael.

The only habitation in view was a ramshackle dwelling, unpainted and dreary, with broken windows and a sagging verandah. Yet it seemed to be inhabited, for there were flowers in bloom, dingy curtains flapping in the breeze, and a black cat which raced away at their approach.

"Dulce – dulce domum", murmured Michael, as he turned into the gateway. "I didn't think we should come across a joint like this in this great and prosperous land. What about sending a snapshot to the Picture Gallery at Australia House?"

But the words died on his lips. The gate was old and broken, but a painted name-board still hung upon it. And the name-board said "Pinelands".

Michael afterwards realised that he was still behaving like a stunned ox, and muttering "But this can't be Aunt Julia. This is all rot ..." when Peter was through the gate, and walking along the weed-grown path, and knocking at the door. And in the moment of time that followed the knock, it seemed to Michael as if the birds hushed their singing, and the sun stood still in the sky.

The door was opened by a policeman. His large figure filled the dingy doorway: he had a forbidding air of authority, and his mouth was twisted into a grim line.

He said brusquely: "Well, and what can I do for you?"

Michael heard Peter say: "We are looking for Mrs. Julia Hope, but this doesn't seem right. Can you tell me if there is another Pinelands in the district?"

The policeman's look passed from Michael to Peter, and back to Michael again, before he spoke.

"This is the Pinelands you are looking for", he said at last. "What is your business with Mrs. Hope?"

"She is our aunt", replied Peter.

"Then I am sorry to tell you that Mrs. Hope was found dead by a neighbour this morning. The doctor is of the opinion that she died suddenly from heart-failure. I am waiting for an ambulance. You had better come in. This has been a shock, I'm afraid".

"Yes", said Peter.

They walked into a room of bleak and cheerless poverty: an uncovered table stood unevenly on broken floor-boards: a dusty dresser with broken doors: a pair of cheap and rickety chairs: a few wooden boxes ranged along the walls: a kettle standing on cold ashes – and that was all ...

"Pete", said Michael. "It's a nightmare. What's it all about? We only heard from her a couple of months ago. How could she have lost everything in that time?"

"Can't you see?" said Peter miserably. "She never had it". He stood by the window and stared out at a glorious panorama: green paddocks rolled down to the red roofs of the little township, and wooded hills stretched beyond it to the horizon. "At least", he thought, "she had this!"

Behind him, Michael and the policeman were laying bare the sorry details of Aunt Julia's life. Their words floated around him, filtered into his understanding through a haze of pity. That fellow – that Australian soldier – in some way must have let her down. No one knew anything of her marriage. She had always been "Mrs. Hope", always alone. Her coming had long been forgotten, and no one knew her business. She was close. If anyone tried to sound her out, they got such a taste of her sharp tongue that they didn't try again! She worked, of course, for her living – worked by the hour, washing sheets at the doctor's house, turning out rooms at the Bank. She would never speak to anyone if she could help it. She would never eat a meal at any house. She had a reputation for being a little mad. She dressed oddly, and spoke strangely. Impudent girls would laugh behind her back as she walked hurriedly down the street.

"And all that time" thought Peter, "she was writing us those letters – on expensive note-paper. She sent me a tie last Christmas – and those food-parcels. They must have cost her hours of charing!"

She had been found, the policeman was saying, lying dead in her chair at the table. She had been about to write a letter. Her note-paper was laid out, and here was the pen she had dropped.

"And look" said Michael. "Here is the note we posted in Melbourne the other day!"

Peter's eye caught a few words: "… May we come up and visit you …" Those words had shattered her card-castle; those words had probably shattered her brave heart too.

"I wish it had been lost in the post," he said.

Well, there was one thing he could still do for Aunt Julia. Michael had disappeared into the inner room where he was presumably helping to make an inventory. Peter sat down at the table, and picked up a sheet of paper. "My dear Mother", he began – and after that Aunt Julia's pen took full command of the situation. Suiting itself admirably to Peter's letter-writing style, it launched itself into an account of his aunt's fatal illness, attended by two famous specialists from Melbourne; of her funeral, and the long procession of cars which followed it; of the flowers, the wreaths and the crosses, the moving address at the Church service, and the grief of a whole neighbourhood.

Now a delicate problem arose – the suitable disposal of a large and flourishing sheep-station, together with several children and grand-children – in such a way that none of them should be heard of again. But the pen was equal to this too.

"Pinelands is to be sold immediately", Peter found he was writing. "Everything is left absolutely to our cousins and their kids – ripping little kids, I promise you! And they feel they must make a complete break. They are probably going to Queensland ..."

It was done – sealed, stamped and addressed.

"I've done what I could, Aunt Julia", said Peter – and he broke the pen in half, and threw it into the ashes.

The policeman came in and said gravely:

"The ambulance is coming up the road. Would you like to help?"

And Aunt Julia went out of Pinelands for the last time.

The Irish-Australian Connellys

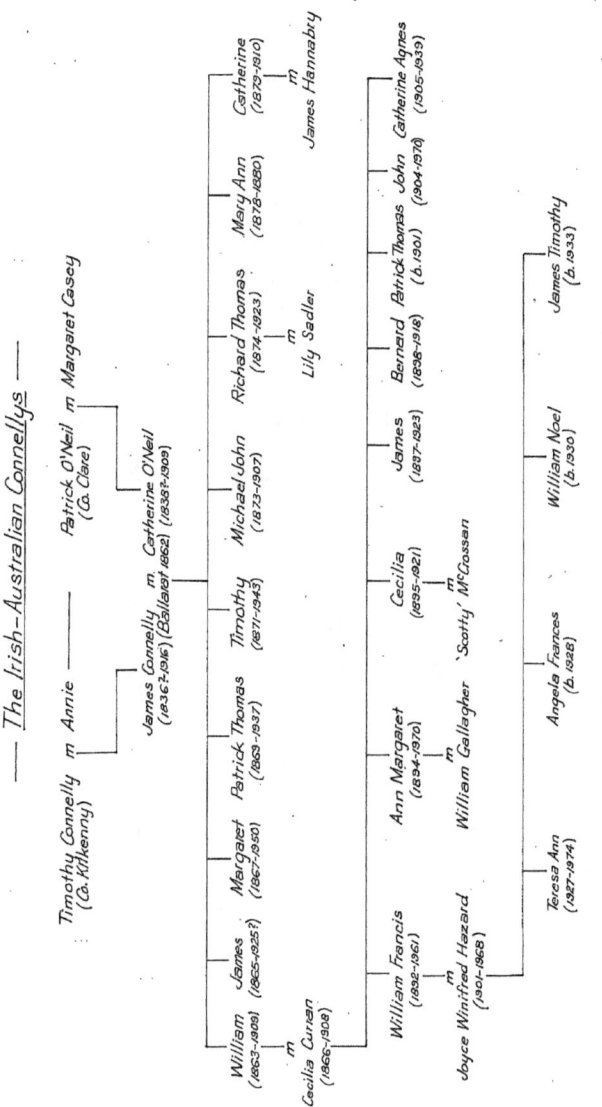

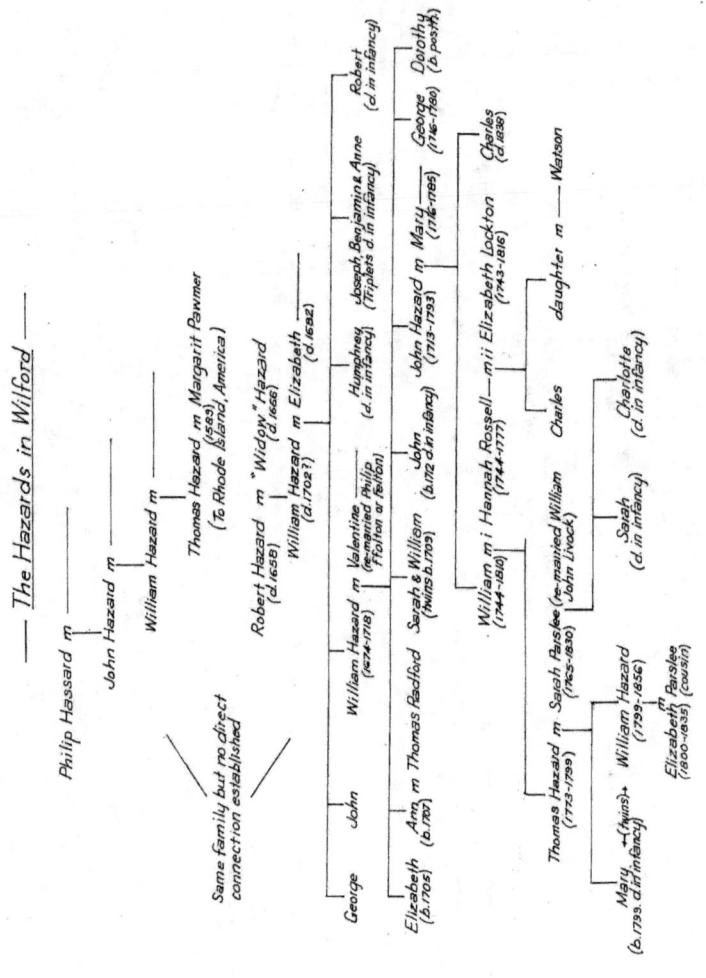

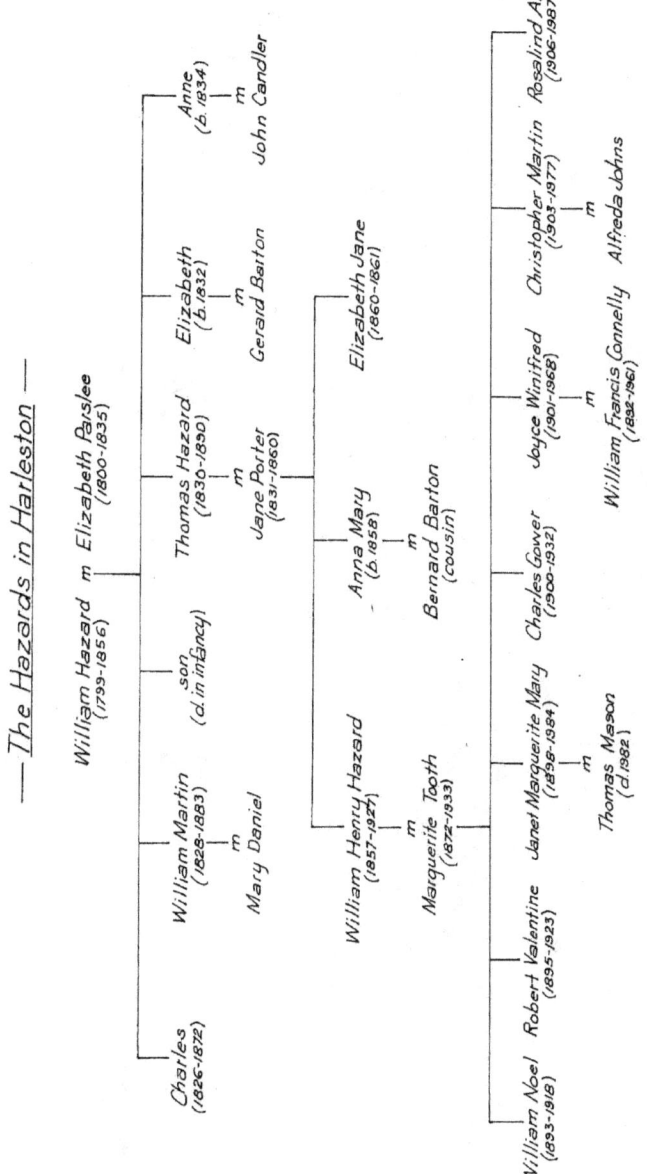

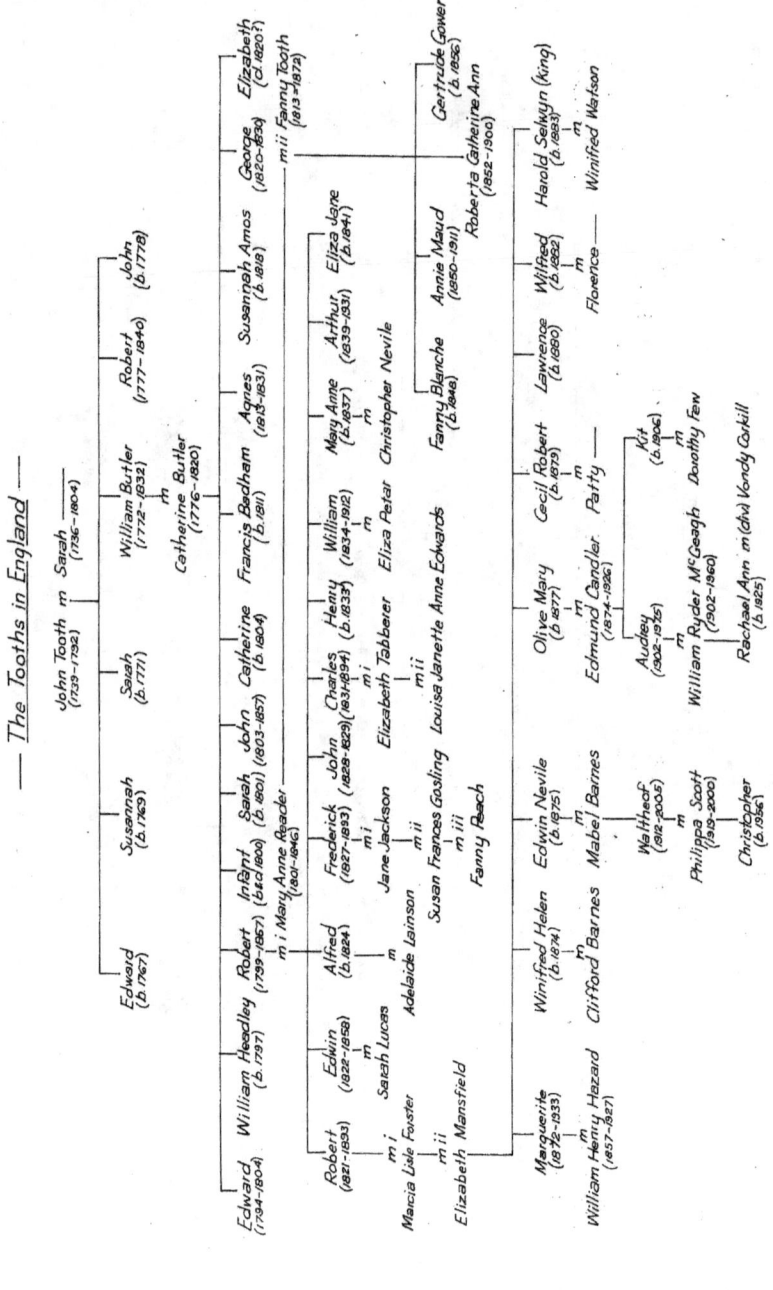

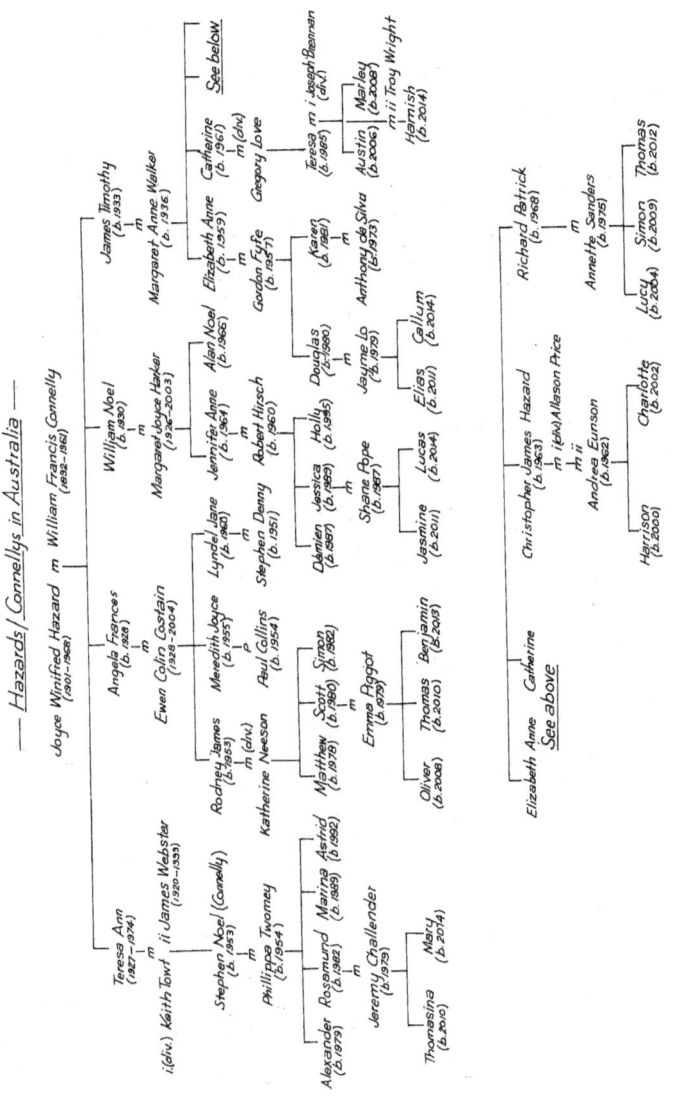

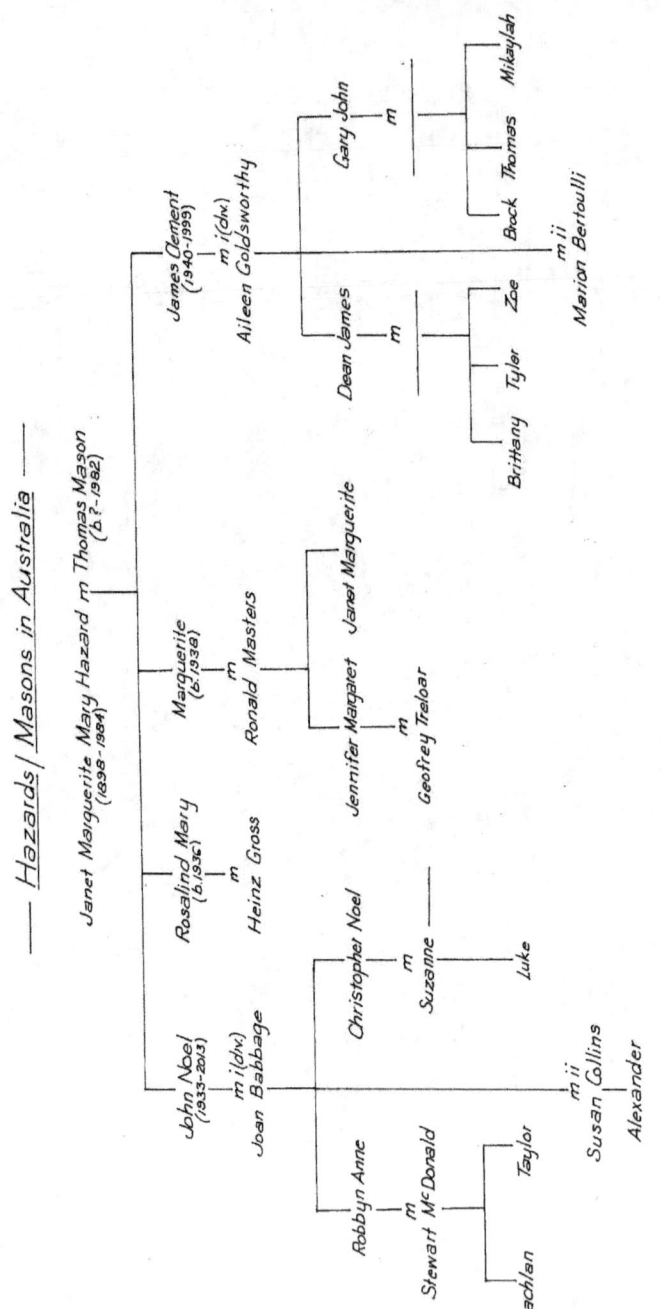

www.ingramcontent.com/pod-product-compliance
Lightning Source LLC
Chambersburg PA
CBHW071906290426
44110CB00013B/1293